Aerobic and Anaerobic Training in Soccer

– special emphasis on traning of youth players

Fitness Training in Soccer I

Buckinghamshire College Group
Wycombe Campus

Publisher: Stormtryk, Bagsværd.
Editors Jens Bangsbo & Ylva Hellsten
Photos:
Per Kærbye: 19, 32, 34, 39, 49, 53
La Press: 54, 61, 70, 72, 76, 80, 93, 99, 109,
112, 141, 150, 152, 155, 182, 185, 188, 197
ISBN: 87-90170-21-0
Printed in Denmark

Aerobic and Anaerobic Training in Soccer

Fitness Training in Soccer I

Institute of Exercise and Sport Sciences
University of Copenhagen
Denmark

Foreword

World Cup 2006 proved that top class football today is a game for highly trained athletes. Even at lower levels, the quality of the game is dramatically effected by the fitness of the participants. In other words, the technical/tactical aspects of the game cannot be divorced from the physical capabilities of the players – consequently, the science of training has become synonymous with the art of the game.

Dr Jens Bangsbo, the author of this excellent book, is truly an expert in his field. He is a football man and a sports scientist – someone who can simplify the mystic of fitness theory and at the same time provide practical guidance to the trainer/coach. In this volume, he provides the reader with an excellent source of reference on training, development, and planning. This is a book which will be of great value to both coach education students and to working technicians; in particular, because the fundamental theory is linked to practical training examples.

Jens Bangsbo has worked for Juventus FC, the Danish FA, for top clubs, and for UEFA and FIFA. He is acknowledged and respected by the football community, including the professionals. As the Technical Director of UEFA, I am pleased to support Jens, and to endorse his new publication: Aerobic and Anaerobic Training in soccer. It will certainly find a place in my collection of important reference books.
–

Andy Roxburgh
UEFA Technical Director

Preface

Through the years I have participated in many fitness training sessions, which I afterwards have realised were of little value. This was either due to the training being of limited relevance to football, or due to the improvement gained from the training soon being lost again, as that particular aspect of the training was not maintained. It is important that the fitness training is specific and efficient, since this will allow for a development that is relevant for soccer and for more time to allocate other aspects of the game such as technical and tactical elements. An optimal way to obtain the desired effect is to perform fitness training with the ball mainly in drills and games. It will not only improve the fitness level, it will also develop technical and tactical qualities of the player and they will be highly motivated. During my years as assistent coach for the first team in Juventus FC, I have seen how important this type of traning is. These aspects are also of particular importance when players are only training once or twice a week.

Results from scientific studies can help understand the demands and the limitations of physical performance in football. Such knowledge, combined with practical experience, provides a good basis for planning optimal programmes for fitness training. In 1994 I attempted to take this approach in the book „Fitness Training in Football - a Scientific Approach", which is based on the research described in the book "Physiology of Soccer" published the same year. I have been pleased to find that the book has created interest among coaches and it is presently translated to ten different languages. This encouraged me to update and edit part of the material into this book and extend the book with a number of new aspects including a chapter about „Development and training of youth players".

The book covers the basic requirements for a coach within fitness training, corresponding to the UEFA B license. For the UEFA A level, knowledge within muscle strength training, muscle endurance training, flexibility training, testing, nutrition and fluid intake is a further requirement. These aspects will be covered in future books „Specific Muscle Training in Soccer", „Fitness Testing in Soccer" and „Nutrition in Soccer". My hope is that this book and the following ones will help to bridge the gap between science and practice, and that it will improve preparation for matches and fitness training in football.

I would like to take the opportunity to thank the coaches and the players, including the players in Juventus and the Danish National team, for their great effort in the numerous studies performed. Furthermore, I want to extend
my
gratitude to all the individuals that have collaborated with me in the scientific studies that form the basis material of the books. Also, I want to thank Ylva Hellsten, Institute of Exercise and Sport Science, University of Copenhagen, Denmark, for her great help with the editing of the book.

Football is not science –
but science may improve the level of football.

Jens Bangsbo, December 2006

Content

Introduction

Anyone who observes a soccer match can recognise that soccer is a physically demanding sport. But how do the players cope with the physical requirements? How should the players prepare for a match? In recent years an extensive number of scientific studies have provided a substantial amount of information with regards to these issues. This book combines scientific results with practical experience in order to give the reader an understanding of the basic principles of how fitness training can prepare the players for a game.

In order to cope with the physical requirements and to maintain the technical standard throughout a match, it is important that the players have a high level of fitness. Playing matches regularly helps to maintain the fitness level of a player, but additional fitness training is required. The training should be specific to soccer, with an emphasis on performing exercises with a ball. Involving the ball during practice ensures that the muscles used in soccer specifically are trained and it also elevates the motivation of the players. It furthermore allows for efficient use of often limited training time, as also technical skills are practised and tactical knowledge is developed.

In the first four chapters, principles of fitness training are discussed in general terms, with practical suggestions on how to organise and conduct training. Considerations are made for all types of players, from recreational players, who train a couple of times a week, to full-time professionals. Specific consideration is given for the development and training of the young soccer player. Fitness training should be based on the fitness level and the specific competencies of the actual group of players, as well as of the individual player. Furthermore, in order to cover all aspects of training in soccer it is important that fitness training is well integrated into the overall training programme.

The following chapters describe aerobic and anaerobic training. This terminology may not be familiar to the reader, but the terms are thoroughly explained and only used for the purpose of separating the different training forms. Within each of the chapters a number of training drills and exercises are given to illustrate the training principles. The different components of fitness training should not be given the same priority all year around. The last chapter "Planning of the Season" describes how fitness training may be varied throughout the year as well as during the week.

The aims of this book are to help the reader understand and utilise fitness training principles, as well as to provide guidelines for achieving effective match preparation. By combining this knowledge with experience about a specific group of players, a well-structured training can be attained, thus benefiting both the coach and the players.

Figure CF1

The figure illustrates how oxygen (O_2) from the atmosphere is transported to a muscle. Air containing oxygen is inhaled through the mouth and passes via the trachea to the lungs where the oxygen diffuses into the blood. When the heart beats, blood carrying oxygen is transported to the muscle. The oxygen is used by the muscle for production of energy, and the by-product carbon dioxide (CO_2) is transported via the blood back to the lungs and removed from the body during exhalation.

Characteristics of fitness training

Fitness training can help a player endure the physical demands of soccer and to maintain the technical abilities throughout a match. Every soccer player over an age of around 14 years, regardless of standard of play, can benefit from a fitness training programme.

This chapter describes in general terms the basic categories of fitness training in soccer. In order to obtain a basic understanding of the principles of fitness training, a brief description of how energy is produced in soccer is also provided. Furthermore, a brief overview of the physical demands in soccer is given, since this forms the basis for fitness training in soccer.

Energy production

Energy is needed in order for the muscles to function. Energy can be formed either with or without the use of oxygen. These two major energy systems are described below.

Energy production with oxygen (aerobic)

When breathing in (inhaling) air, which contains approximately 21% oxygen (O_2), flows into the lungs. Some of the oxygen in the lungs diffuses into the blood and is then transported to the muscles and different organs of the body. The oxygen transport system consists of lungs, heart, blood vessels and blood (see Fig. CF1). The right half of the heart pumps blood low in oxygen to the lungs to replenish the blood with oxygen. The oxygenated blood then flows to the left half of the heart. When the heart muscle contracts (heart beat), the blood is then pumped to all parts of the body via blood vessels. When the blood arrives at a muscle it flows into smaller blood vessels (capillaries) where some of the oxygen and nutrients, such as carbohydrate and fat, in the blood, are liberated for use by the muscle fibres. Within the muscle, the nutrients are broken down chemically in a process that requires oxygen, resulting in the release of energy (see Fig. CF2, page 14). Because oxygen is used, the process is termed aerobic energy production (aero = air). One of the byproducts of this energy production is carbon dioxide (CO_2), which is transported by the blood to the lungs where it is removed during breathing out (exhaling; Fig. CF1).

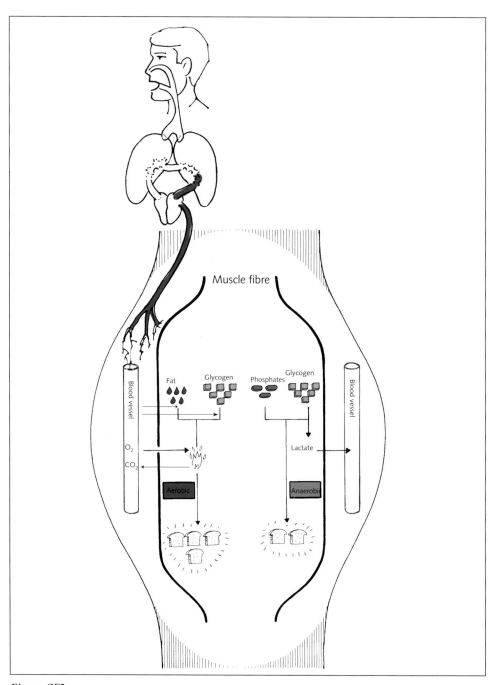

Figure CF2

The figure shows how energy is produced in the muscles through aerobic and anaerobic processes. For aerobic energy production, oxygen (O_2) is utilised in processes in which fat and carbohydrate (glycogen) are used. Anaerobic energy production does not require oxygen and proceeds either through the breakdown of high-energy phosphates stored in the muscle, or by the use of carbohydrate (glycogen) with the formation of lactate.

14

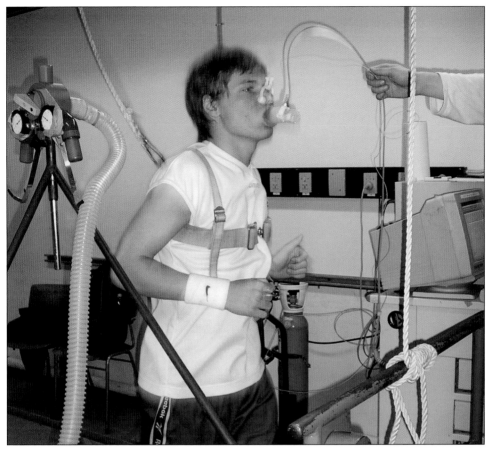

A player's maximum oxygen uptake can be determined by collecting exhaled air during running until exhaustion on a motor driven treadmill. The volume of air is measured and the content of O_2 and CO_2 in the air is determined.

The amount of oxygen that the body uses per minute is termed oxygen uptake. At rest the oxygen uptake is about 0.3 l/min. During exercise the oxygen uptake is higher than at rest and increases with increasing exercise intensity. However, the capacity to transport and utilise oxygen is limited. The largest amount of oxygen that can be used per minute by the body is termed maximum oxygen uptake. For healthy individuals, the maximum oxygen uptake is within the range of 2 to 7 l/min. More energy, and thus oxygen, is needed to move a heavier body. To make comparisons between individuals of different sizes, the value for maximum oxygen uptake may be divided by the body weight. By this calculation, an individual who weighs 80 kg and who has a maximum oxygen uptake of 4 l/min will get a value of 50 ml/min/kg. Another individual with the same absolute maximum oxygen uptake, but with a body weight of 60 kg, will have a value of 67 ml/min/kg.

Figure CF3 shows the average and range of maximum oxygen uptake (expressed as ml/min/kg) for Danish top-class male (see Fig. CF3A) and female players (see Fig. CF3B) in different positions. The maximum oxygen uptakes of the Danish players are similar to values obtained from other top-class players in Europe.

Energy production without oxygen (anaerobic)
The transport of oxygen to the muscles is not always sufficient to enable energy demands to be met entirely by aerobic energy production. This applies especially to the beginning of exercise where there are rapid changes in energy demand and during high intensity exercise. In such cases the muscles also produce energy through processes which do not require oxygen. These are called anaerobic energy processes (an = non, aero = air).

Small energy stores (high-energy phosphates) present in the muscles can rapidly make energy available through anaerobic processes (see Fig. CF2, page 14). Energy can also be produced at a high rate from the anaerobic

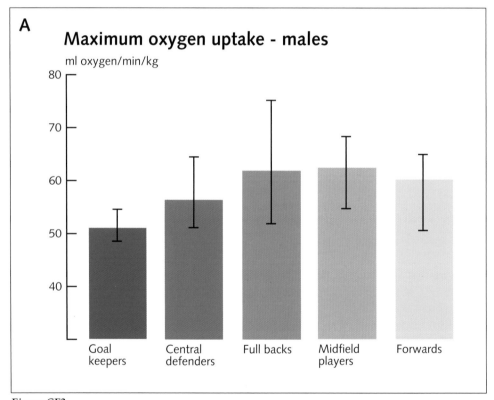

Figure CF3
The figure illustrates the average maximum oxygen uptake and range, expressed as ml oxygen/min/kg body weight for (A) 82 male and (B) 20 female top-class Danish soccer players in different positions. The maximum oxygen uptake of the male and the female soccer players was significantly higher than that of non-trained individuals, but considerably lower than that of elite endurance athletes such as long-distance runners who have values around 85 and 75 ml/min/kg for males and females, respectively.

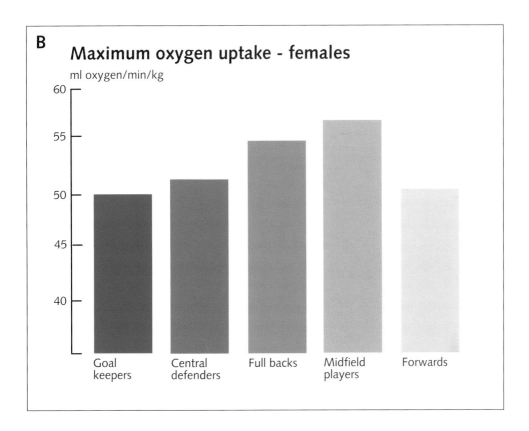

B

Maximum oxygen uptake - females

ml oxygen/min/kg

breakdown of carbohydrate (glycogen), where a substance called lactate is formed as an end product. During high intensity exercise, lasting longer than a few seconds, a large amount of lactate is produced.

Some of the produced lactate in active muscles is released into the blood, while the remainder accumulates within the muscles and can be used as a fuel to produce energy in the presence of oxygen (see Fig. CF4, page 18). As the intensity of exercise is increased, more lactate is produced, leading to higher and higher muscle and blood concentrations.

Lactate released from the muscles is transported via the blood to the heart. Here, the blood from the muscles is mixed with blood from less active areas of the body, which have a lower lactate concentration. Thus, the lactate concentration in the blood leaving the heart is lower than that of the blood flowing directly from the active muscles to the heart. As the heart pumps blood around the body, it is possible to measure raised lactate concentrations in blood taken from the arm, even if it is the leg muscles that have produced the lactate. However, the lactate concentration in blood taken from the arm or fingertip provides only limited information about the amount of lactate produced, as the lactate in mixed blood has been diluted and because some lactate is used as fuel by the exercising muscles and other tissues (see Fig. CF4, page 18).

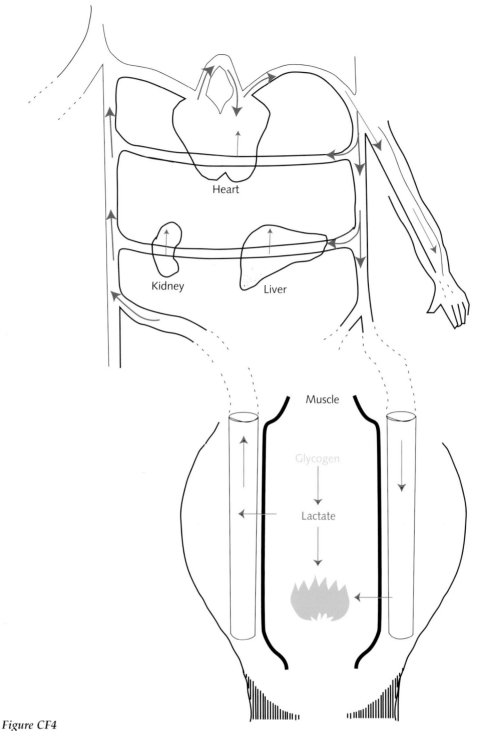

Heart

Kidney

Liver

Muscle

Glycogen

Lactate

Figure CF4

The figure illustrates the fate of lactate produced in the muscles. Some of the lactate remains in the muscle where it either accumulates or is used as a substrate for aerobic energy production. Lactate released into the blood is transported to the heart, which pumps it around the body, and various tissues, such as the heart, liver, and kidneys, absorb lactate from the blood. A small proportion of the lactate is transported to the arms. It is therefore possible to measure elevated lactate concentrations in blood sampled from the arm, even though exercise has been performed with the legs.

Lactate is highly produced during the intensive parts of a game.

Requirements of the game

Soccer is a physically demanding sport. It has been shown that a top-class male soccer player covers a distance of about 11 km during a match and makes approximately 1300 changes in exercise intensity (see Fig. CF5). The time a player is in possession of the ball is, however, limited to a few minutes per game.

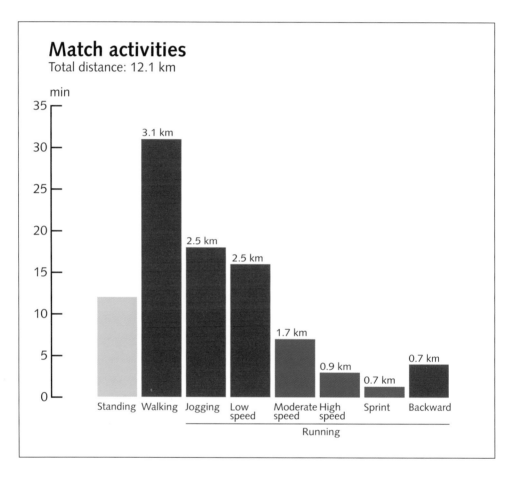

Figure CF5

The figure shows the activities of a French top-class midfield player during a competitive match. The values are expressed both in minutes and in distance (kilometres) covered during the different activities. As an example, moderate speed running accounted for 7 minutes, thus corresponding to a distance of 1.7 kilometres (7 minutes x 15 km/hour).

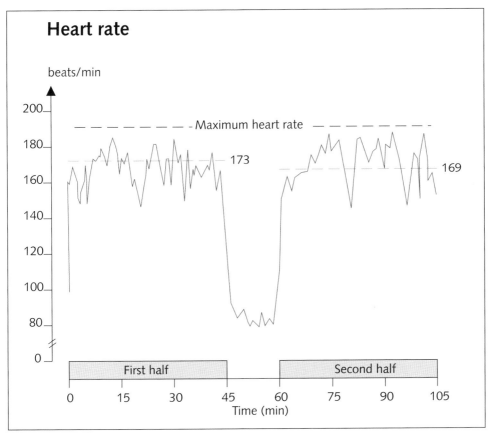

Figure CF6
The figure shows the heart rate of a player during a match. The maximum heart rate for the player and the average values for first and second half are also given.

The aerobic energy system provides by far the greatest amount of energy used during a match. This is illustrated by the relative high heart rates during a soccer game (see Fig. CF6). Heart rate and body temperature measurements indicate that a top-class player exercises at an average intensity of approximately 70% of maximum oxygen uptake. Such high exercise intensity, maintained for 90 minutes, places high demands on the oxygen transport system and the endurance capacity of the muscles.

Anaerobic energy production is important because it is needed for periods of high intensity running and other strenuous activities, such as tackling, turning, and jumping. During a match, a top-class player performs about 30 sprints that, on average, last about two seconds. The energy production

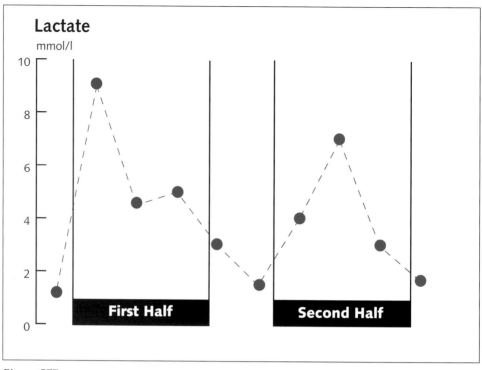

Figure CF7

The figure shows blood lactate concentrations for a player before, during, and after a match. The values varied greatly during the match ranging from 1.5 to 9 mmol/l*

for these sprints is derived primarily from the anaerobic breakdow of high-energy phosphates, which are regenerated during a subsequent rest period. During periods of high intensity exercise, energy is also provided by the anaerobic lactate producing processes, as is indicated by high blood lactate concentrations during match-play (see Fig. CF7).

Well-developed co-ordination and a high strength level in certain muscle groups, in particular the leg muscles, is advantageous for a soccer player.

Types of fitness training

At low exercise intensities, the muscles produce energy almost entirely from aerobic processes. During high intensity exercise the aerobic energy production is limited and a substantial part of the energy used is supplied by anaerobic processes (see Fig. CF8).

*The unit „millimoles" (mmol) indicates a certain quantity of a substance. This unit is practical to use within the disciplines of chemistry because it allows substances to be compared. In a resting state the lactate concentration in both muscles and blood is around 1 mmol (per kilogram of muscle and per litre of blood, respectively) which corresponds to an absolute quantity of 90 milligrams.

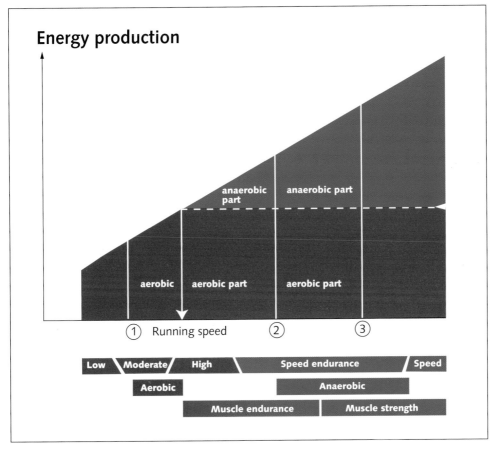

Figure CF8
The figure shows energy production at different running speeds. At low running speeds (e.g. the speed indicated by ① most of the energy is produced aerobically. At the speed indicated by the vertical arrow, the limit of energy production from the aerobic system is reached (maximum oxygen uptake – indicated by the dotted line) and at higher speeds the remaining energy is produced anaerobically. The figure shows two running speeds ② and ③ with the same aerobic energy production (i.e. maximal) but with a different anaerobic energy production.

At the bottom of the figure the various components of fitness training are positioned according to energy production during training.

Low = aerobic low-intensity* training, Moderate = aerobic moderate-intensity training, High = aerobic high-intensity training, Speed endurance = speed endurance training, Speed = speed training, Muscle endurance = muscle endurance training, Muscle strength = muscle strength training.

* Exercise Intensity: Work performed per unit of time. For example, if player A runs 1 km in 5 minutes and player B runs the same distance in 10 minutes, then player A has exercised with an intensity (speed) twice as high as that of player B.

Based on the energy pathway that is dominant, fitness training in soccer can be divided into a number of components (see Figs. CF8 and CF9).

During a match or a training session, a player's exercise intensity varies frequently. In some periods energy is provided almost exclusively via the aerobic system, while at other times a large proportion of the energy is produced via the anaerobic systems. Figure CF10 (see page 26) shows examples of how exercise intensity can vary during games and drills within aerobic and anaerobic training. Some overlapping exists between the two categories of training, e.g. the exercise intensity during aerobic high intensity (Aerobic$_{HI}$) training may, in some periods, become as high as during speed endurance training.

The separate components within fitness training are briefly described below.

Aerobic training

Aerobic training can be divided into aerobic high-intensity training, aerobic moderate-intensity training, and aerobic low-intensity training (see Fig. CF9).

A soccer player should be capable of exercising at high intensities at any time during a match. The ability to perform this type of exercise can be improved through aerobic high-intensity training. It is also important that a player is able to maintain a high physical and technical standard throughout a match. Therefore, a part of the training should aim at improving the capacity to exercise with varying running speeds for long periods of time (endurance). By performing aerobic moderate-intensity training the endurance capacity of a player can be increased. On the day following a match, or after several days of intensive training, a player may need to recover, which can be done by performing light physical activities – aerobic low-intensity training.

Anaerobic training

Anaerobic training can be divided into speed training and speed endurance training (see Fig. CF9).

An average sprint during a match lasts less than three seconds. However, as a sprint may be important for the final outcome of a match, it is advantageous for a player to perform speed training. In soccer, speed is not merely dependent on the physical capacity; it also involves fast decision making which must be translated into quick movements. The aim of speed training is to improve a player's ability to perceive, evaluate, and act quickly in situations where speed is essential.

During a short sprint (1-5 seconds), energy is produced primarily through breakdown of phosphates, but the lactate producing anaerobic system is also important. During longer periods of high-intensity exercise energy is produced mainly via the latter system. High blood lactate concentrations measured from top-class players during match-play indicate that the lactate producing energy system is important in soccer and should therefore be specifically trained. This can be achieved through speed endurance training, which improves the capacity to repeatedly perform high-intensity exercise.

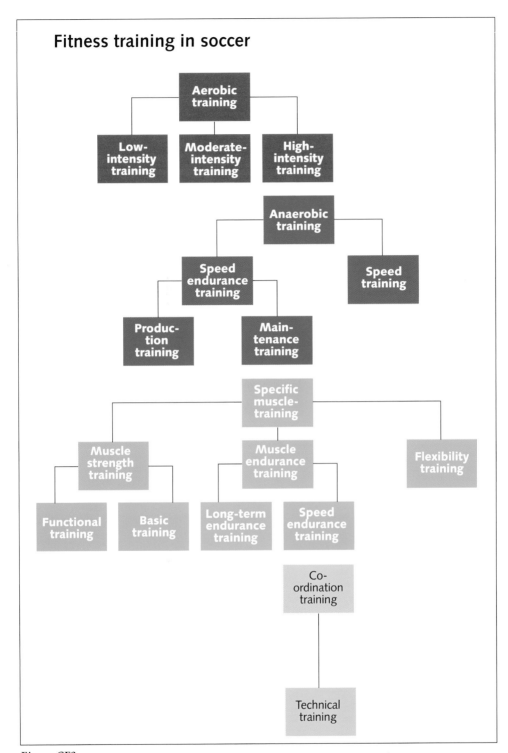

Figure CF9
Components of fitness training in soccer.

25

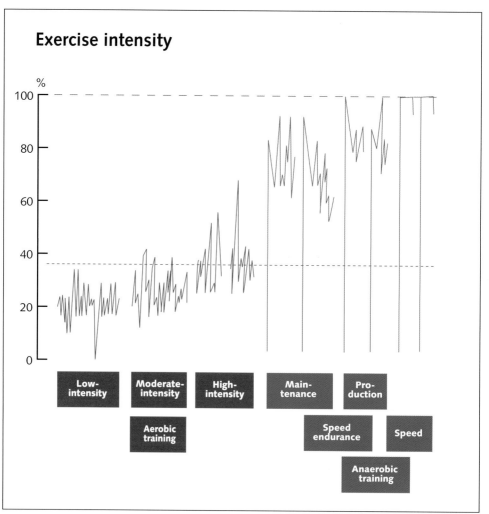

Figure CF10
Examples of the exercise intensities (expressed in relation to maximal intensity (100%)) of a player during games within aerobic and anaerobic training. Some overlap exists between the categories of training, e.g. the exercise intensity during aerobic high intensity training may in short periods become as high as during anaerobic speed endurance training.
The exercise intensity eliciting maximum oxygen uptake and the maximal exercise intensity of the player are represented by the lower and the higher horizontal dotted line, respectively.

Muscle speed enderance traning can easily be performed on the field.

Specific muscle training

Specific muscle training involves training of muscles with isolated movements. The aim of this training is to increase performance of a muscle to a higher level than can be attained solely by playing soccer. Specific muscle training can be divided into muscle strength, muscle speed endurance, and flexibility training (see Fig. CF9, page 25).

Training biceps using some form of external resistance, e.g. dumb-bells, is an example of a form of muscle strength training. Training the abdominal muscles using several repetitions of an appropriate exercise is an example of muscle endurance training. Stretching the hamstring muscles is an example of flexibility training.

Training methods

A major part of fitness training in soccer should be performed with a ball, since such training has several advantages:

● The specific muscle groups used in soccer are trained.

● The players develop technical and tactical skills under physical demanding conditions similar to those encountered during a match.

● This form of training usually provides greater motivation for the players compared to training without the ball.

When training with a ball, however, the players may not work hard enough, as many factors, such as tactical limitations, can lower the exercise intensity. To increase the demands of a training game new rules may be introduced (see page 87).

When a soccer field is unavailable the coach should be as creative as possible when organising a training session. An example of a good alternative is a heading game, where the players alternately pass the ball with hands and head. In this way the fitness training is performed with movements that are similar to the ones used during a match.

When performing the fitness traning with the ball also tecknical aspects are trained.

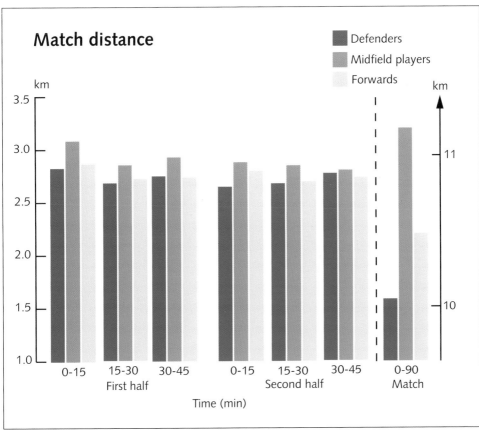

Figure CF11
The figure illustrates distances covered by defenders, midfield players, and forwards during top-class competitive matches. To the left each half of the game has been divided into 15-minute intervals (0-15, 15-30, 30-45 min), and to the right values for the whole game are shown (0-90 min). Apart from the last 15 minutes of the match the midfield players covered considerably more distance than the other two groups of players.

In addition, such games will involve tactical and technical elements, which are relevant to soccer. In that respect much can be gained compared to running without a ball. Under some circumstances it may be necessary to train without a ball. If this is the case the training should mainly be carried out on grass, with the players are wearing soccer boots and performing movements that resembles those during match-play.

Individual training

In soccer, the physical demands of a player during a match are influenced by several factors, such as the player's tactical role (see Fig. CF11) and technical standard. Similarly, the characteristics and the physical capacity of players in the various positions are different. This is illustrated in Figs. CF3 (see page

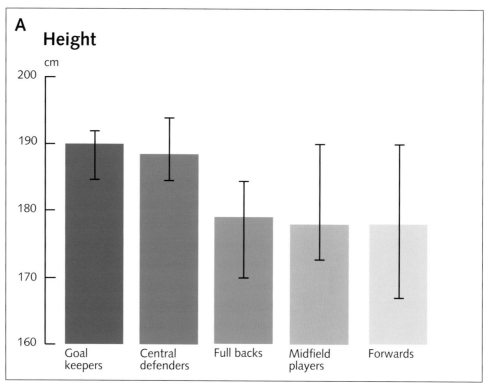

A Height

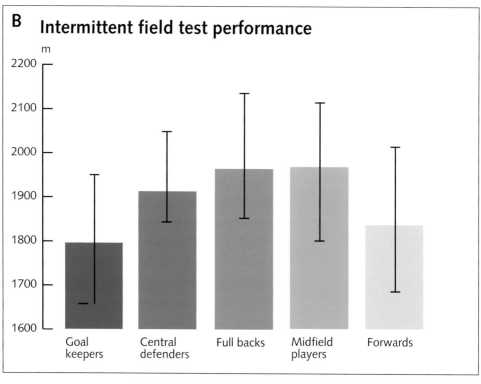

B Intermittent field test performance

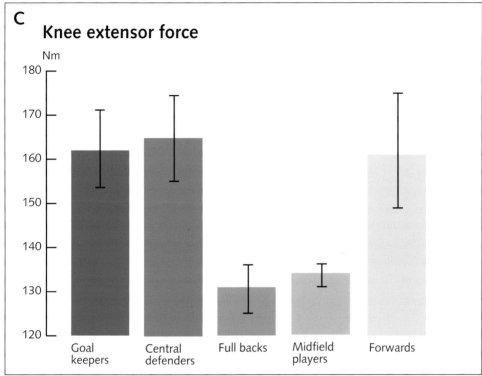

Figure CF12

The figure shows physical characteristics of elite male soccer players in different positions of a team. For each position, an average value as well as the lowest and the highest value (range) are given. (A) Body height, (B) Intermittent field test performance, and (C) Muscle leg strength measured at a velocity of 180 deg/second.

16) and CF12, which represent results from 82 top-class Danish male soccer players. It is clear that the goalkeepers and central defenders were the tallest, whereas the mean height for full backs, midfield players and forwards were the same (see figure CF12A). The full backs and midfield players had higher maximum oxygen uptake and better field test performance than the other player groups (see Figs. CF3 and CF12B), whereas the full backs and midfield players had the lowest strength of the leg muscles (see Fig. CF12C). Within each player category there was a marked variation, showing that even though two players have the same position in a team, they may have very different physical capacities.

It is obvious that players in a team have different training needs. A part of the fitness training may therefore be performed on an individual basis, where the training can be focused on improving a player's strong and weaker abilities. It is important to be aware of the fact that, due to hereditary differences, there will always be differences in the physical capacity of players, irrespective of training programs. This fact is illustrated by results from tests made with players in the Danish World Cup team of 1986. Although all of the players in the team were close to their peak fitness level, the maximum oxygen uptake of the players ranged from 57 to 69 ml/min/kg body weight (the highest value found for a Danish soccer player is 76 ml/min/kg). Players who are physically weaker may be able to compensate through superior qualities in other aspects of the game. This type of player is also needed on a team, and it is important for the coach to chose a playing system and style, which fits the strength of the available players. The strategy of a soccer team is often selected in such a way that players with high physical capacities perform the most work. For instance, midfield players usually possess a high endurance level and run a substantially longer distance than other players during a match. Individual physical demands must be considered when planning fitness training, but the extent of individual training is dependent upon several factors, such as the total training time available. Individual training can be performed in small groups because several players may have the same needs and players can be trained differently in the same game. An example of such training is the game „Position" described on page 14.

Training of female players

The overall exercise intensity in female soccer is not as high as in the male game due to the lower physical capacity of female players. Nevertheless, as a result of the increasing popularity and rapid development of female soccer, greater physical demands are being placed upon female players. The maximum oxygen uptakes of female players is as for male players related to the position in the team and the values are somewhat lower than observed for male players (see Fig. CF3, page 16). However, the activity profile of female soccer is very similar to that of male soccer (see Fig. CF13), and there is little difference in the training potential of men and women, i.e. the response to training from a baseline level is similar. Therefore, male and female players should basically train in the same way and the training advice given in this book is applicable to both genders.

The activity profile of female elite players during a match is the same as that of male top-class players.

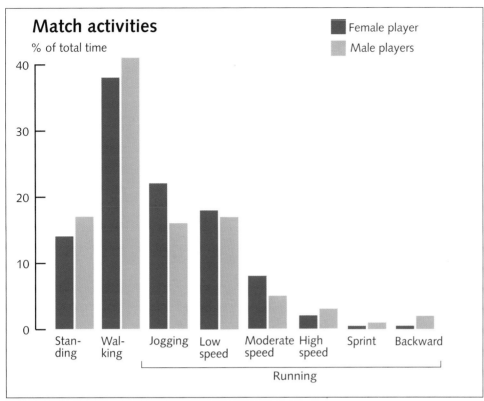

Figure CF13
The figure shows the activities of a top-class female player and male elite players. Note that the pattern of activities are the same for the female player and the male players, but the female player performed less high speed running and sprinting.

It is important to emphasise training at a high intensity for top-class female players. However, as alterations in the menstrual cycle may occur if the training suddenly becomes very demanding, it is advisable to increase the amount and intensity of exercise gradually. If any menstrual changes do occur, the player should either take a period of rest or follow a less demanding training program.

Summary

The performance potential of a player can be improved by fitness training, which can be divided into aerobic training, anaerobic training, and specific muscle training. Common to all types of fitness training is the fact that the exercise performed during the training should be as similar as possible to playing soccer. This is one of the main reasons as to why the majority of fitness training should be performed with a ball.

As a supplement to the general fitness training, exercises may also be designed to accommodate the individual needs of the players. Fitness training for females and males should follow the same principles.

Physical development and training
of young players

Children develop psychologically, socially and physically throughout their childhood as in no other period in life. Thus, a child's ability to play soccer is dependent on social experiences, psychological development and physical capacity. No children are alike. Each child develops individually depending on his or her biological genetic potential, biological maturation and the environment. For example, in a group of 12-years old girls some may, in terms of development, correspond to a 9-year old girl, whereas others may have reached a level of a 15-year old girl.

It is very important as a coach of young players to be aware of the players' development stage and understand how the youth players can be trained to have fun, improve, and not impair their development. Children are not small adults and should definitely not be trained in the same way as adults. In this section, a brief summary of the physical changes occurring during childhood and specific information about children playing soccer will be presented. Furthermore, particular considerations of training of young soccer players will be presented.

Physical development of young players

Both girls and boys may before puberty (approximately age 6 to 12 years) increase their body height by 4-8 cm per year. During a period the rate of growth in height becomes significantly greater (8-15 cm per year) representing the start of puberty (see Fig. PY1, page 36). This period is called the adolescent growth spurt, and the age at which the growth speed peaks is called „peak height velocity " and is abbreviated PHV. There is a variation in the duration of the growth spurt but in most cases it lasts 1-2 years, whereafter the increase in body height becomes smaller and smaller; and the growth may stop at an age around 16 and 18 years for girls and boys, respectively (see Fig. PY1, page 36). The time of the start of the growth spurt gives information about the maturation of the child. The earlier the more mature the child is. There is a large difference in individual maturation within a given age group. The adolescent growth spurt may start as early as the age of ten or it may not start until the age of sixteen. This is illustrated in another way in Fig. PY2, which shows how many girls in different age groups that have their first menstruation (menarche), which is another sign of maturation. It is clear that in a majority of girls onset of menarche occurs at an age between 12 and 14 years, but also that some girls have their first menstruation much earlier and some when they are older than 14 years. On average, girls mature about two years earlier than boys. To express the degree of maturation, the term biological age is used rather than the chronological age, which is the child's age from birth. The first sign of puberty in boys is an increase in testicular volume and in girls, onset of menarche and growth of the breasts. The next phase in maturation is the beginning of growth of pubic hair.

In the period of a growth spurt a child may have difficulties to

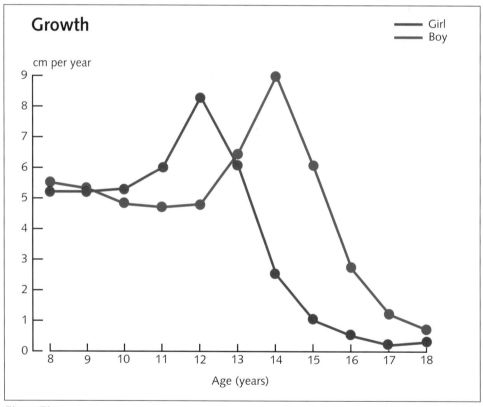

Figure PY1

The figure shows increase in body height per year for a girl (●) and a boy (●). Note that the increase is quite constant around 5 cm per year for both the boy and the girl until a point where there is a marked elevation in the rate of growth, which is called the growth spurt. This occurred about 2 years earlier for the girl than for the boy. After the growth spurt, the increase in body height became smaller and the final height was reached at an age of around 16 years for the girl and around 18 years for the boy.

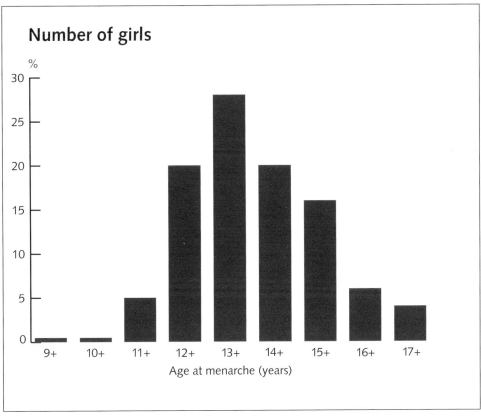

Figure PY2

The figure shows the number of girls, expressed in % of the total number of girls studied, that got their first menstruation (menarche) in different ages groups. 9+ means 9-10 years, 10+ means 10-11 years and so on. It is obvious that about 70% of the girls get their first menstruation between an age of 12 and 15 years, but also that some girls get menstruation at a very early age and some at a rather late age.

co-ordinate movements, since the changes in body dimensions are so rapid. It is common that the children have problems even with simple tasks that they were able to do previously. Boys have more pronounced difficulties than girls as their increase in body dimensions is greater. There is a common perception of „awkwardness" occurring at this period of adolescence. Is should be noted, however, that less than one-third of adolescent children are heavily affected and for all the effects are transient. Playing soccer on a regular basis does not affect statural growth, the timing or magnitude of peak height velocity, nor skeletal maturation.

For both girls and boys the body mass increases in parallel with increasing body height before puberty and for boys body mass continues to increase during puberty. Girls in puberty produce the hormone oestrogen, which increases the amount of fat and they get a relatively greater body weight in relation to height. After puberty, girls have around twice as much adipose tissue as boys of the same height.

Skeleton

Childrens' bones are softer than those of adults as their skeleton contains more cartilage and is more elastic. This means on one hand that children are more flexible and that they are less prone to acute injuries that may occur for example upon falling. On the other hand are children more susceptible to obtain permanent injuries due to erroneous, one-sided or too great physical loading. Not until the age of 20 can the skeleton be expected to be fully developed.

Muscle mass

At birth and early childhood the mass of muscle accounts for about 20% of the body mass. The mass of the muscle in the body increases as children grow (see Fig. PY3). Until puberty the development of muscle mass is similar for girls and boys. During puberty, boys, in contrast to girls, get a marked increase in the hormone testosterone, which leads to considerable growth of the muscles. Also the proportion of muscle mass in relation to body mass increases for boys after sexual maturation and reaches around 40% as adult. It is common to observe that the mass of muscles of boys is doubled from an age of around 10 years to an age of 17 years. In girls the magnitude of muscle mass levels off during puberty (see Fig. PY3).

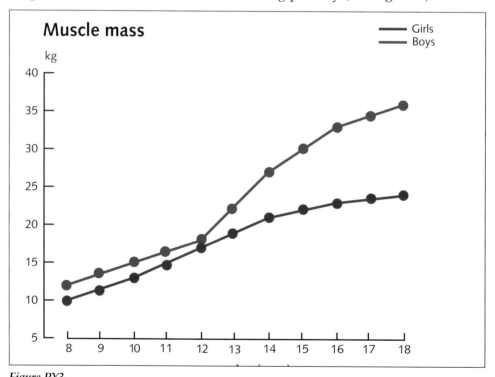

Figure PY3

The figure shows the total muscle mass of boys (●) and girls (●) of different ages. Note that the increase is the same for boys and girls until puberty whereafter the muscle mass of boys increases further whereas there is only minor changes for girls.

Young soccer players develop also their muscle mass through playing.

Aerobic energy production

Before puberty, maximum oxygen uptake increases with increasing age and the change is similar for boys and girls (see Fig. PY4). During puberty the boys have a marked increase in maximum oxygen uptake, whereas the increase is moderate for girls. One reason for the difference is that boys have a more pronounced increase in the specific protein „haemoglobin", which transports oxygen in the blood.

For soccer players maximum oxygen uptake is often expressed in relation to body mass, since performance in soccer is not only dependent on the body's ability to transport and utilise oxygen but also on the mass each individual has to move on the field. Since the increase in maximum oxygen uptake is associated with a parallel increase in body mass as children get older, maximum oxygen uptake per kg body mass is not changing much for boys (see Fig. PY5). For girls it decreases at puberty since the increase in body fat is not associated with an increase in maximum oxygen uptake (see Fig. PY5). In general, children playing soccer have significantly higher maximum oxygen uptake than children of the same age not participating in sport.

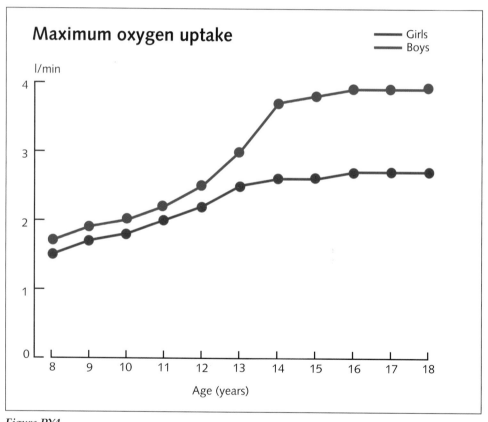

Figure PY4

Maximum oxygen uptake expressed as litre of oxygen taken up per minute for boys (●) and girls (●) in different age groups. Note that the increase is the same for boys and girls until puberty whereafter the boys have a further development of maximum oxygen uptake with no changes for girls.

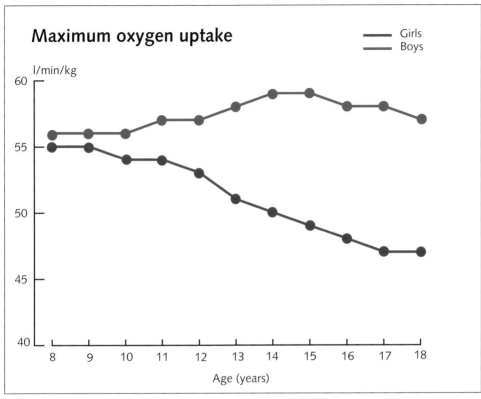

Figure PY5
Maximum oxygen uptake expressed as litre of oxygen taken up per min per kg body mass for boys
(●) and girls (●) in different age groups. Note that that there are very small changes for boys
whereas the girls have a major decrease during puberty due to a significant weight gain caused by an
elevated mass of adipose tissue.

Anaerobic energy production

Unlike for maximal aerobic power expressed per kg body mass, in which children are on a par with adults, children have significantly lower maximal anaerobic power and capacity. Anaerobic performance, irrespective of gender, is closely related to muscle mass of the growing individual and both anaerobic power and capacity increase progressively during maturation until reaching adult levels after the teenage years (see figure PY6, page 42).

Development of running speed accelerates in two phases. The first is at about 8 years in both sexes, which is related to the maturing of the nervous system and improved co-ordination of arm and leg muscles. The second occurs at an age of about 12 for girls and between 12 and 15 for boys.

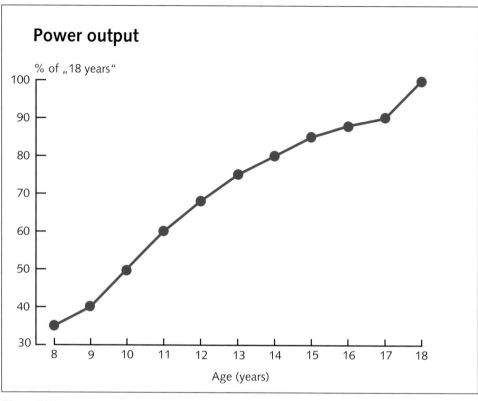

Figure PY6
The figure shows the anaerobic power of the legs of boys (●) of different ages in relation to performance at an age of 18 years (100%). Note that boys at an age of 8 years only have an anaerobic power corresponding to 35% of that at an age of 18 years and that there is a marked development throughout the childhood, but mostly in ages below 13 years.

Muscle strength

The power produced during a maximal movement is closely related to the mass of the muscles involved in the movement and therefore follows the development of muscle mass as children grow (see Fig. PY7). Until puberty, the development of muscle strength in the legs is the same for girls and boys, whereas from an age of about 6-7 years the strength in the upper body is higher for boys than for girls. One of the reasons may be that boys are more active with the upper body than girls. The development in muscle endurance, which denotes the ability to sustain high mechanical power over time, e.g. 30-60 s, follows a similar change as muscle strength.

The development of muscle strength is also associated with an increased performance in activities requiring a high power output. Figure PY8 (see page 44) shows that the ability to jump, both for boys and girls, increases in association with increases in muscle mass and muscle strength (see Figs. PY3 and PY7).

Perception and co-ordination

A child's ability to co-ordinate movements is a combination of maturation, training, genetic and environmental factors. At an age below 10 years most children will not be able to perform complex movements, since the nervous system is not sufficiently developed. The child will also have difficulties to evaluate speed and direction of a ball as well as position in relation to other players (perception). It is common to see the ball hit the player rather than the player hitting the ball. Maturation of the nervous system is related to the chronological age and at an age of around 12 years perception is usually fully developed, which means that the players can perceive and evaluate, but they may not be able to control a complicated movement. At that age children are able to learn technical elements, which after a period of training will be performed automatically, i.e. the child performs the movement without being conscious. At every stage of development, children can perform some movements automatically, whereas some movements still

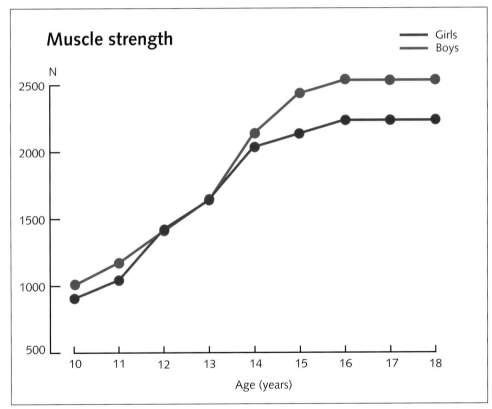

Figure PY7
The figure shows muscle strength of the legs of boys (●) and girls (●) of different ages. Note that the muscle strength increases in a similar way in boys and girls until an age of around 14 years, whereafter the girls only have a moderate rise, in contrast to boys that continue with an increase in muscle mass.

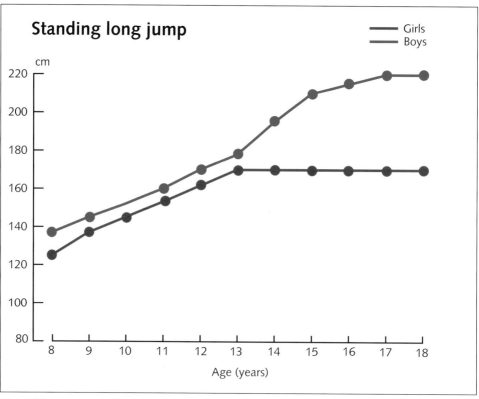

Figure PY8
The figure shows performance in a standing long jump for boys (●) and girls (●) of different ages. Note that jump performance develops in a similar way in boys and girls until an age of around 13 years, whereafter performance of the girls is unaltered in contrast to the boys who have a marked further increase.

need a high degree of concentration and there are a substantial number of movements they can not perform.

A young player's ability to learn a technical detail is also dependent on how mature the player is. It is wrong to try to teach a child a complicated movement if the child has not yet developed to a level where it is possible to learn such a movement. It may, in contrast, lead the child to loose self-confidence. Therefore, it is important that the coach of young players is aware of the developmental stages and degree of maturation of each player, and is able to support the players also in periods with no development.

An easy way to get a rough measure of the level of motor control for a child is to perform a balance test as shown on Fig. PY9. The test result is the number of attempts that is needed to stand on the balance bar for one minute in total. In scheme PY1 some reference values for soccer players at the ages of 10-14 years are given. Is should be emphasised that the test does not give a complete picture of the players' ability to co-ordinate movements.

| | Age (years) | |
	11-12	13-14
Good	<5	<3
Average	5-15	3-12
Below average	>15	>12

Scheme PY1
The scheme shows reference values of a balance test for soccer players. The test result is the number
of attempts to maintain the balance for a total of one minute.

Figure PY9
Test at a balance bar (50 cm x 3 cm). The player captures balance while holding a person, as soon as
the player stands alone the clock it started and the clock is stopped when the player looses balance
and falls off the balance bar. The player then gets up again and continues until he/she in total has
been on the balance bar for one minute.

Training of young players

Youngsters should not be viewed simply as miniature adults and training programs used by adult teams should not be transferred to them. When training young players one should be aware of that there is a large difference in individual maturation within a given age group. Another important aspect of youth training is the amount and intensity of training. The coach should carefully observe how the individual players respond to the training, as young players can easily be „overloaded". The child's habitual activity should also be taken into account, since for most youth players the majority of time playing soccer lies besides the organised training. In this section, the effect of training of young soccer players on various aspects of physical performance will be presented. Specifically the development of players at different competitive levels and the selection of young elite players will be considered.

Aerobic and anaerobic training
Children and youths are adaptive to aerobic and anaerobic training as long as the training stimulus is adequate. However, as described above, before puberty and during puberty the players have a natural development of aerobic and anaerobic performance and young soccer players get a sufficient physical improvement by regular participation in drills and games. This is

Through playing in a small area young soccer players develop their technical qualities and fitness level.

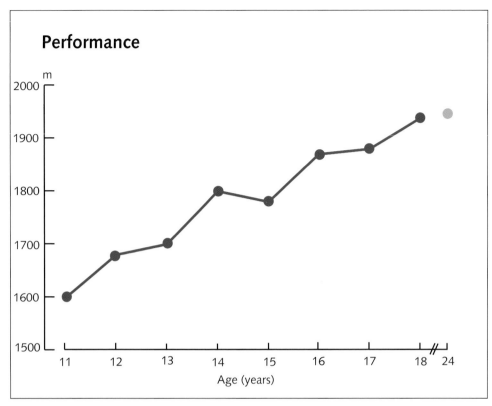

Figure PY10

Running distance during an intermittent field test (performance) for youth players (●) and adult elite players (●). Note that the players at the early ages had a marked improvement, although there was no focus on fitness training and that the 18 year old players had a performance similar to top-class players (average of 24 years).

also clear from a Danish study with 132 young players from three different soccer clubs that did not practice fitness training with players under 15 years of age. The players were tested using a soccer-specific endurance test (see the book "Fitness Testing in Soccer"). The results from the different age groups are shown in Fig. PY10 and can be compared to results for 82 senior players playing in the Danish league. For the boys younger than 15 years there was a pronounced increase in performance with age despite the fact that they did not perform any specific fitness training. Furthermore, the results of the 18-year old players were as high as those of the top class players. This demonstrates that a player can reach a top-class level as senior player without performing fitness training during the younger years.

At the end of puberty, the players can start performing drills for development of their aerobic and speed performance. Drills within anaerobic speed endurance training should not be performed until after puberty, i.e. when players are older than 15 years.

Strength training

Strength training can result in substantial increases in strength for children. The strength gains in pre-adolescents, especially during the early stages of strength training, are mainly attributable to an increase in neuromuscular activation, i.e. part of the strength gain may simply reflect improved motor co-ordination. This means that the effect is rapidly lost and it is also clear that a group of players performing strength training will after a period of training converge towards and reach the level of players not taking part in the strength training. Thus, training-induced strength gains during pre-adolescence are impermanent for players before and during puberty. Also, considering that strength training is an activity that may induce temporary or permanent musculoskeletal injury, there are no valid arguments for performing strength training for young soccer players.

At the end of puberty, the children may start to perform functional strength training, consisting of exercises where a player's own body is used as resistance. Not until after puberty should the players should perform basic muscle strength training using power machines and free weights. These types of equipment should only be used under supervision and with appropriate technique instruction (for further information see the book „Specific Muscle Training in Soccer").

Training of co-ordination

Many of today's greater athletes in ball games are characterised by having spent a lot of time in sport and having participated in different sports as youngsters. Such extensive and varied activities have developed the whole body co-ordination of the players. It has also been recognised that young soccer players playing at the highest level at an age of 10 are better co-ordinated than players at the same age playing at a lower level. It not only relates to co-ordination of the legs but also in movements where legs and arms have to be co-ordinated. It is clear that young soccer players can benefit from obtaining experience of a broad range of physical activities to stimulate whole-body co-ordination. Such an experience will form an important fundament for the technical development and will make the players able to be in a good balance and rapidly handle changes in movements occurring during a game. Training of young players should, therefore, include activities where several muscle groups are involved such as take off, rolling, feint, turns, rotations and other specific exercises using a ball, focusing on the co-ordination between upper and lower body. Soccer players may also play with their hands and heads every once in a while. For example basketball or „headball", where the players alternate throwing and heading the ball (the player with the ball can only take three steps). In general, most important is that young soccer players get as much contact with the ball as possible. Therefore, almost all training for youth players, including the „warm-up" (see page 55), has to be performed with balls. It can be obtained by playing small-sided games with a limited number of players. The majority of the games described in this book can be used, if the playing space is significantly reduced and in some cases also the number of players.

Young players improve their fitness level by the training with the ball and by playing games.

Maturation and selection

A Danish study with more than 100 young soccer players has focused on the development of soccer players playing at the highest level (elite), i.e. members of the first team, and a lower level (non-elite) from an age of 10 years. It was clear that both elite and non-elite players had a significant development of the oxygen transport system (maximum oxygen uptake) and muscle strength as well as of co-ordination skills (see Fig. PY11).

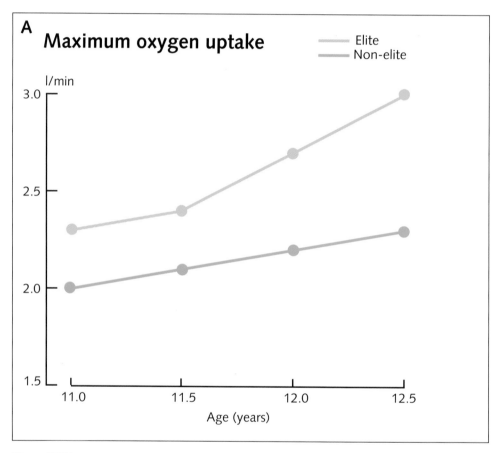

Figure PY11

The figure shows physical characteristics of young soccer players selected for the best team (elite, ●) and playing at a lower level (non-elite, ●). (A) Maximum oxygen uptake, (B) Muscle leg strength (both legs), and (C) Co-ordination abilities measured as time to complete given exercises combining legs and arms; the shorter the time the better the performance. Note that the elite players had better performance than the non-elite players already at an age of 11. Furthermore, both groups improved as they became older, but the increases for the elite players in the last phase became greater than for the non-elite players.

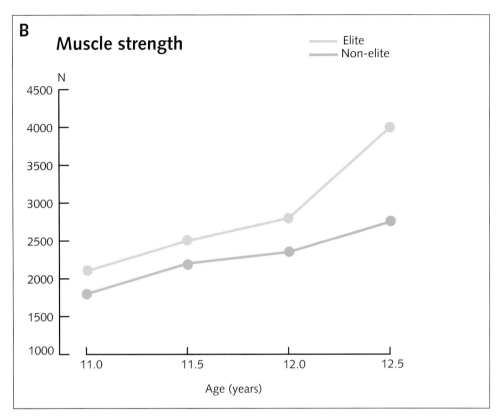

B

Muscle strength

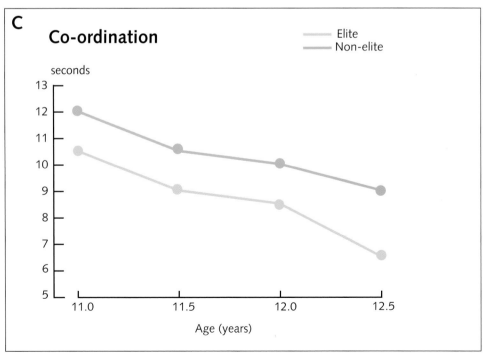

C

Co-ordination

The elite players were more mature than the non-elite players, and they had superior physical capacities already at an age of 10-11 years. It is likely that some of the players were selected for the first team due to these abilities, which is supported by the observation that the majority of the elite players were born in the first 3-months of the year (see Fig. PY12). The same has been shown to be the case in Holland, England and Sweden, where the youth national teams had an over-representation of players born in the early months of the selection period. Even at the senior national team level the majority of players were born in the first half of the year, which may be a result of these players being more mature as youngsters and therefore being selected and receiving the best training. There is good evidence that the performance advantage of early matures disappears at an adult age. Thus, as maturation status can have a profound effect on physical performance, care should be taken not to underestimate genuine soccer talents due to physical immaturity in comparison with the other players in the same age group. Talented players that are not yet as developed physically as their age matched team-mates should also have the opportunity to train optimally. Otherwise quite a number of talents may be lost.

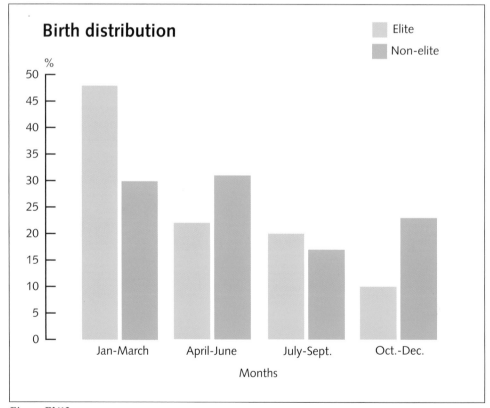

Figure PY12
The figure shows the relative number of players at an elite and non-elite level born in four periods of a year. Note that more elite than non-elite players are born in the early part of the year.

Young player developing his tecnical skills.

Summary

When training young soccer players it has to be recognised that:

- Children have a constant and balanced development from start of playing soccer until start of puberty (onset of growth spurt).

- There is a great variety in the onset of puberty among children and that the effect of puberty on the ability to play soccer varies greatly between young players.

- Almost all training should be performed with the ball.

- Prior to and during puberty, training of the players should not be focused on the physical aspect, but should mainly emphasise the co-ordination and technical aspects.

- At the end of puberty, the players may also start to perform aerobic training and speed training and to a limited extent functional muscle strength training.

- After puberty, the players can carry out basic muscle strength training and muscle endurance training.

Warm-up and recovery activities

This chapter outlines general principles of warm-up and recovery activities following a match and a training session.

Warm-up

Every match and training session should be preceded by a period of warm-up since it allows a player to gradually adapt, both physically and mentally, to the subsequent exercise.

Aims

- To increase performance.

- To decrease the risk of injury.

Effects

During exercise the active muscles produce heat. As the intensity of the exercise increases more heat is generated. Some of the heat is transferred from the muscles into the blood and is dispersed throughout the body. Thus, exercising with large muscle groups not only causes an increase in muscle temperature, but also results in a considerable rise in body temperature. During intense exercise the muscle temperature may rise to 43 °C while body temperature can reach 41 °C.

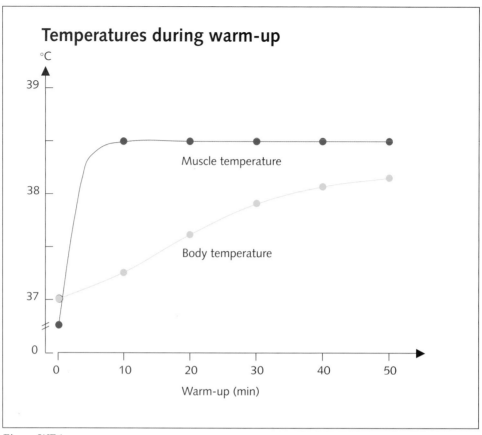

Figure WR1
The figure illustrates the changes in body (◯) and muscle (●) temperature during 50 minutes of exercise. The body temperature increased gradually, whereas the muscle temperature only increased during the first 10 minutes, whereafter it remained constant.

Figure WR1 illustrates what happens to the temperature of muscle and body during a warm-up. The muscle temperature reaches a stable level after about 10 minutes, whereas the body temperature is still rising after 50 minutes. A rise in muscle temperature increases the ability of the muscle to produce energy during exercise. This is one reason for the improvements in performance observed after a warm-up. Figure WR2 shows the relationship between muscle temperature and performance during a brief sprint on a cycle ergometer. From the results in Fig. WR1 and WR2 it can be concluded that a warm-up should last for at least 10 minutes in order for the players to fully benefit from the increase in muscle temperature.

Many injuries occur due to an insufficient warm-up. A cold muscle is relatively rigid and resilient to sudden increases in tension caused by rapid movements. When the elastic components of the muscle are unable to accommodate the external tensions, the muscle will rupture. This is commonly referred to as a „pulled" muscle.

Application to soccer

Every training session or match should begin with a warm-up. In addition to the physical effects, the warm-up also has psychological benefits. Before a match it may help some players to control their nerves and concentrate on the match. For training, a warm-up can stimulate the players and prepare them mentally for the work ahead.

Organisation

The exercise intensity should be low at the beginning of a warm-up and gradually increase. The tasks should be technically easy to perform; otherwise there is a risk that the overall activity level will be too low, and the warm-up will not have the desired effect. A warm-up should also include light stretching exercises (see page 72).

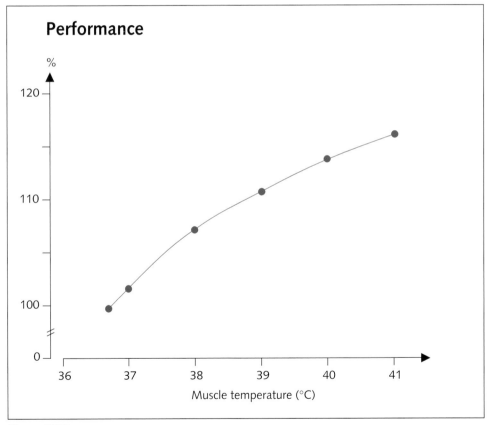

Figure WR2
The figure illustrates the relationship between muscle temperature and sprint performance. The higher the muscle temperature, the better the performance, e.g. at a muscle temperature of 41 °C performance was 15% greater than at 37 °C.

Both weather and temperature must be considered when planning a warm-up. When the air temperature is high, the temperature of the muscles and body increases rapidly and less time for warm-up is needed. Nevertheless, some warm-up exercises need to be performed to obtain a sufficiently high muscle temperature. In cold weather it is advisable that the players wear extra training clothes to decrease the loss of heat from the body, and to enable the muscle and body temperature to increase more rapidly.

Towards the end of a warm-up performed before a match the exercise intensity should be high (see Fig. WR3). This is not necessary for a warm-up during training since the coach and the players can control the exercise intensity of the subsequent training drills. Other differences between warm-up for match and training are discussed below.

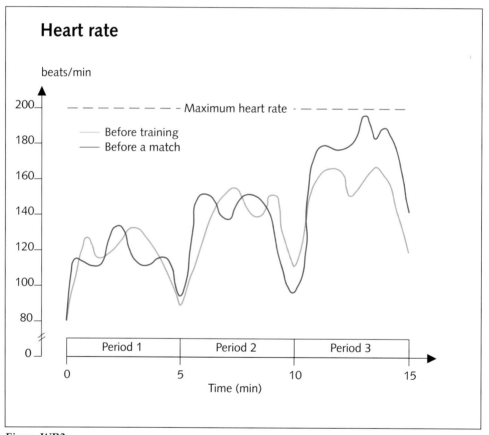

Figure WR3
The figure shows heart rate for a player during a warm-up before training (———) and prior to a match (———). Heart rate varied by approximately 25 beats/min within each of the three five-minute periods, and on average heart rate increased from one period to the next. Towards the end of the warm-up prior to the match, heart rates reached almost maximal value, whereas the values at the end of the warm-up before training were considerably below maximum level.

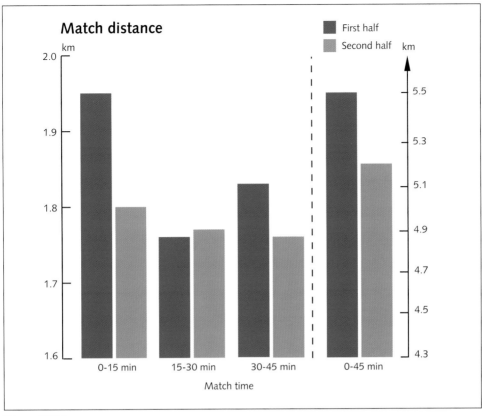

Figure WR4
The figure shows distances covered in the first and second half of a match. To the left each half is divided into 15-minute intervals (0-15, 15-30, 30-45 min) and to the right the two halves (0-45 min) are compared. The players covered a longer distance (around 300 meters) during the first half compared to the second half. Note that the distance covered at the start of the second half was significant shorter than at the first 15 min of the game.

Pre-match and half-time warm-up

After cessation of exercise, the temperature of the previously activated muscles decreases quickly and is back to a pre-exercise level after approximately 15 minutes. A warm-up before a match should therefore continue until the start of the match. In top-class soccer the players often return to the changing room after the warm-up and stay there for more than 15 minutes. During this time many of the benefits gained during the warm-up are lost. If the break is short (e.g. five minutes), however, the loss in muscle temperature can in part be regained by performing some activities immediately before kick-off.

A considerable decrease in muscle temperature does also occur at half-time. It has been observed that the running distance in the beginning of the second half is markedly shorter than that of the same period in the first half (see Fig. WR4). One possible explanation for this difference is a decrease in muscle temperature during the break. Thus, in a recent scientific study it was demonstrated that the sprinting ability of players is reduced at the start of the second compared with the end of the first half. This was associated with a decrease in muscle temperature of about 2 degrees Celsius. Therefore, it is advisable that the players perform some kind of activities at half-time and do a short re-warm-up (5-7 minutes) before the second half, especially when the break lasts more than 10 minutes. When a group of players followed such a procedure, they had the same sprinting capacity at the start of the second half as before the game.

It is important to be aware of the psychological value of warming up prior to a match. The players should be allowed to do part of the warm-up on their own. For example, directly after changing, before a more structured team warm-up, and then again just before the start of a match. An important element of the pre-match warm-up is that the players work with a ball, so that they will have a feel for the ball prior to the game. In a warm-up before a match, 15 minutes could be spent to accommodate individual needs, followed by a warm-up for the team lasting 10 minutes and ending with five minutes for the players to exercise on their own.

Pre-training warm-up

When planning a warm-up programme for training the coach should try to be creative. To achieve an effective and motivating warm-up programme, almost all the exercises should be performed with a ball. It is common to regard warming up as an isolated activity with the only purpose to increase the muscle and body temperature. The result is a poor utilisation of an often limited time for training. Instead, the warming up can be used to repeat and further develop technical and tactical elements. It is important, however, that these aspects do not require a long introduction, since the effect of the warming-up will be compromised.

To decrease the risk of injury, the warm-up should be initiated with some exercises that activate large muscle groups, for example jogging with or without a ball, before playing against opponents. After approximately five minutes of whole body exercises, light stretching exercises can be performed. The warm-up should then be continued with exercises for the main muscle groups used during soccer, which can be achieved by playing a „passive" small-sided game. After another series of stretching exercises the intensity of the warm-up activities can be increased. An example of the fluctuation in heart rate of a player during a pre-training warm-up programme is shown in Fig. WR3 (see page 58).

Below a number of examples of warming-up drills are given. They are simple to organise and allow for training of technical and tactical aspects. The drills can be used at all levels of soccer. To motivate and to make improvements, the exercises within a drill should be chosen so that they challenge the players' tactical and technical performance.

Warm-up before a match can be performed both individually and in groups.

Warm-up 1 – Collaboration (Fig. WR5)

Area:

A soccer field with two penalty areas and a middle circle.

Number of players: 20 (3-30).

Organisation:

Each second player has a ball. The players start in one of the penalty areas.

Description:

The players with a ball are dribbling in the penalty area and the players without a ball are jogging in between. When a player with the ball gets „eye-contact" with a player without a ball, they run towards each other and they make a „take-over", i.e. the player without a ball continues with the ball.

When the coach points at the middle circle, the players with a ball have to dribble and the other players have to run to the middle circle, where they continue performing „take-overs". After a period, the coach points at either of the penalty areas and the players run to that penalty area, and so on. The activities can be changed to train other tactical and technical elements (for detailed description of tactical aspects see „Attacking Soccer", by Bangsbo & Peitersen, Human Kinetics). For example:

Tactical elements
● Wall-pass: Upon „eye-contact" the player with a ball passes to the other player, who returns the ball in a correct wall pass. After a period of time the players without a ball get the ball.

● Overlap: A player without a ball is running at a high speed from behind, passing a player with a ball who, as the player pass, plays the ball and the other player is continuing with the ball.

● Run in free space: Upon „eye-contact" the player without a ball increases the running speed and runs to a free space where he receives the ball from the other player.

Technical elements
● The pass to the other player has to be a specific kick, e.g. instep.

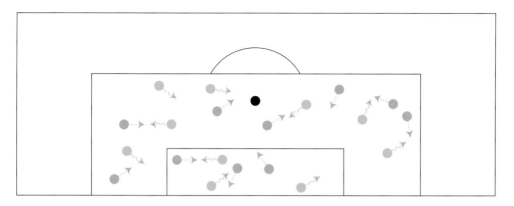

Collaboration (Fig. WR5)

● The ball is passed in the air and returned with a header. After a period of time the players without a ball get the ball.

● The ball is passed in the air and the player receiving it stops it with the chest (or thigh/foot), controls it and continues with it.

Advanced
● The players with a ball pass a player without a ball and when the players' have reached a distance of around 5 metre, the player with the ball passes it to the other with a heal-kick.

End of warm-up
● The players that do not have a ball should try to get one and the other players are defending their ball. When running between the penalty area and the middle circle the players can also capture a ball.

Hints for the coach:
This warming-up drill allows the players to repeat and train also tactical and technical details. Both the tactical and technical tasks should be chosen so that they are rather easy for the players to perform to avoid that the players have to stop the warming-up for a prolonged time. The instructions should be limited and mainly consist of coaching while the players are performing the exercises. The players should in the beginning dribble and run at a moderate speed. As the warming up progresses the intensity should be enhanced, in particular when dribbling and running between the penalty areas and the middle circle. The coach can control the overall intensity by the frequency of the runs between the penalty areas and the middle circle; the more runs there higher the intensity. The intention of the coach pointing when the players have to change zone, is to train the players ability to perceive when doing a technical or tactical detail. The players should not look at the coach all the time, but rather react when some of the other players start to run towards the other zone.

Warm-up 2 – Technical (Fig. WR6)

Area: A soccer field with two penalty areas and a middle circle.

Number of players: 20 (3-30).

Organisation: Each player has a ball. The players start in one of the penalty areas.

Description: The players are dribbling between each other. When the coach points at the middle circle all players are dribbling to the middle circle, where they continue dribbling between each other. After a period the coach points at either of the penalty areas and the players run to the indicated penalty area, and so on. Below are provided some examples of technical elements , which the players can perform in various time periods.

- Dribbling only with one foot (left/right), dribbling only with the inner or the outer side of the foot. Running backwards dribbling with the sole of the foot. Dribble five metres then turn and dribble five metres and then turn.

- The players are making various faints either decided by the coach or themselves. They can also do a specific faint when they are dribbling against one of the other player (both players do the same faint).

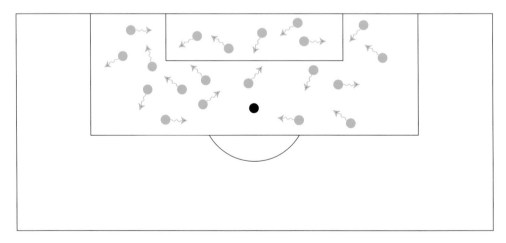

Technical (Fig. WR6)

- At a given signal each player puts first the right and then left knee on one ball and then continues to another ball. In total they may touch four different balls, whereafter they continue dribbling. The players can do other activities related to the ball, such as jump five times over the ball or take five steps with each foot on the ball.

Advanced
- Juggling the ball in a certain way, e.g. shift between foot and thigh, left and right leg or leg and head.

- Get the ball in the air with one foot and do a header and stop the ball, or kick the ball in the air about 3 metres forward and stop it, thereafter relaxed dribbling and then again kick the ball in the air and so on.

End of warm-up:
- The players should try to kick the ball of the other players out of the area without loosing control of their own ball. When the ball is kicked out of the area, the player loosing the ball has to run at a high speed to get it, whereafter he has to dribble back to the area.

Hints for the coach: This warming-up drill allows the players to repeat and train technical details. The technical tasks should be chosen so they are rather easy for the players to perform to allow the players to work all the time. Thus, the technical instructions should be limited and mainly consist of advice while the players are dribbling. In the beginning, the players should dribble at a moderate speed. As the warming up progresses the intensity should be enhanced, in particular when dribbling between penalty area and middle circle.
The coach can control the overall intensity by the frequency of the runs between the penalty areas. The intention of the coach pointing when the players have to change zone, is to train the players ability to perceive when doing a technical or tactical detail. The players do not have to look at the coach all the time, but rather react when some of the other players start to run towards the other zone.

Warm-up 3 – Pairs (Fig. WR7)

Area: Half a soccer field.

Number of players: 20 (2-30).

Organisation: The players are together in pairs, i.e. 10 pairs. One of the players (1) is standing with the ball at the midline, and the other is positioned about 5 metres from his partner (2).

Description: The players start passing to each other (which they do everytime they are at the midline). The players can move closer and closer to each other, and then further and further away from each other (while still passing the ball to each other). It can be required that the players use a specific way of kicking such as instep, wrist and/or they have to kick with a certain foot (left/right). On a signal player 1 is running forwards and player 2 is moving backwards. The players are still passing to each other. At the next signal 2 runs forwards and 1 is running backwards while the players are still passing to each other. When 1 reaches the midline both players stop running and pass to each other. Instead of passing when running a number of different technical actions can be made such as:

- The player running backwards has the ball in the hand and throws the ball at the other player to head back, or to play back in the air with the inside of the foot or wrist (left or right foot), or to stop with the wrist, thigh or chest and then pass back.

- 2 plays the ball with the foot rather than throwing it, or the players can keep the ball in the air with exactly one, two or three touches.

  Progression
- 1 passes 2 in a dribble whereafter 1 plays the ball with the heal to 2. Then 2 dribbles and passes 1, whereafter he plays with the heal and so on.

- 1 plays the ball to 2, who turns around and dribbles with the ball until 1 in high speed passes 2, then 2 plays 1, who slows down so 2 in high speed can pass 1 and receive the ball, and so on.

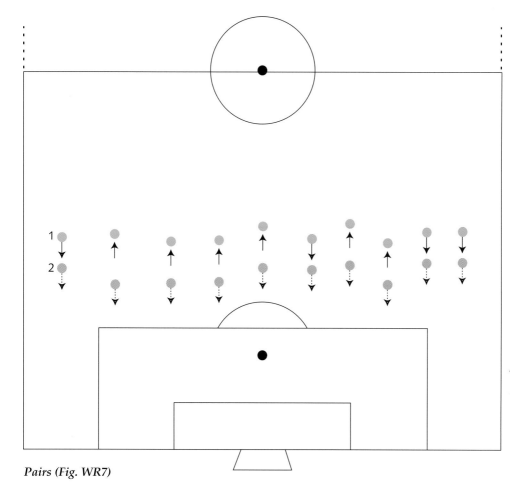

Pairs (Fig. WR7)

Advanced

- 1 plays the ball over the head of 2, who turns around and runs after the ball, while 1 is running in the direction of 2. When 2 gets the ball he turns around and plays the ball over the head of 1, who runs after the ball and so on.

Hints for the coach: It is important that the players are active also in the periods of passing to each other at the midline. The technical elements have to be carefully selected not to lower the overall intensity. If the ball is kicked away the player not running after the ball should run back and forth until his partner is back. The intensity should be progressively increased which can be done by introducing the changes described in „Progression" or by doing other types of activities with the ball. The coach should be coaching the execution of the technical elements.

Warm-up 4 – Playing (Fig. WR8)

A warm-up programme with the ball for 24 players including two goalkeepers is described below. The programme consists of three phases during which the exercise intensity is gradually increased. It lasts approximately 30 minutes, but can be shortened by excluding parts from each of the three phases.

Phase 1 (6 minutes)
a. The players are together in pairs (two goalkeepers are working together) and they are running back and fourth on the field. They are passing to each other. Passing can be replaced by alternatives such as dribbling with take-overs or overlapping. The total duration of this phase could be around five minutes.

b. The players are given one minute to gently stretch, maintaining each stretched position for only a few seconds.

Phase 2 (12 minutes)
A soccer field is divided into a number of zones (they can not play in the shaded zones; see Fig. WR8). The players are together in groups of six, with ten zones for every six players.

a. Four players play against two players (4v2), with the two players trying to touch the ball. If one of the two players successfully touches the ball, this player then changes places with the player who made the mistake. A ball kicked out of the playing area is also regarded as a mistake. The players can only play in one zone at a time. If the ball is "played into another zone, all the players should go to this zone before the ball can be passed into a new zone. Total duration of the game is approximately five minutes.

b. A three-a-side game (3v3). Each team is trying to keep possession of the ball. One point is scored if a team can make 10 consecutive passes without the other team touching the ball. As in a. the players are only allowed to play in one zone at a time. Total duration of the game is approximately five minutes.

c. The players perform light stretching exercises for approximately two minutes.

Phase 2

a.

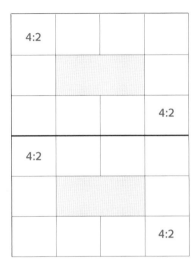

b.

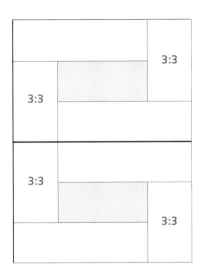

Phase 3

a.

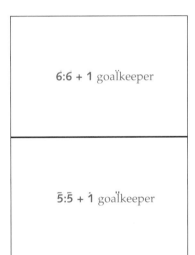

b.

Playing (Fig. WR8)
The figure shows the organisation of phases 2 and 3 of the warm-up programme described in the text.
There are 24 players including two goalkeepers. In phase 2 each part of the field is divided into ten
zones. In the first part (a) four players play against two (4v2), and in the second part (b) three
players play against three (3v3). In phase 3 the field is divided into four zones of equal size. In the
first part (a) six players play against six (6v6) on each half of the field, and in the second part (b) six
players play against six (6v6) with one goalkeeper on one half of the field, and five play against five
(5v5) with one goalkeeper on the other half of the field.

Phase 3 (12 minutes)

a. The field is divided into four zones of equal size (see Fig. WR8). The players are together in groups of 12, with two zones (half the field) per 12 players. A six-a-side game (6v6) is played with each team trying to keep possession of the ball. A point is scored if 10 successive passes can be made without the other team touching the ball. As before, the players must only play in one zone at a time. Total duration of the game is approximately five minutes.

b. A six-a-side game (6v6) in one half of the field and a five-a-side game (5v5) in the other. There is a goalkeeper in each half. A point is scored for passing the ball to the goalkeeper who must catch it and then throw it to a player in the same team. Total duration of the game is approximately five minutes.

c. The players stretch for around two minutes, holding each stretched position for 10-15 seconds.

Different drills with a ball can be used for warm-up.

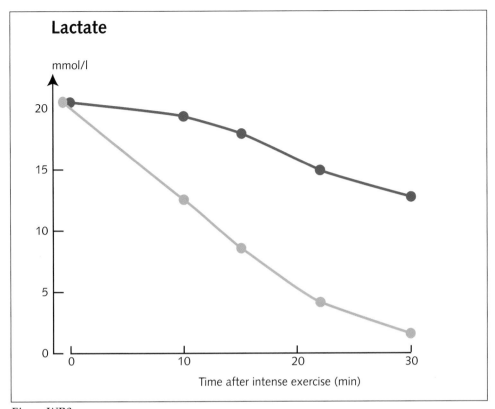

Figure WR9

The figure shows the blood lactate concentration after intense exercise followed by either »active« (jogging, ●) or »passive« (●) recovery. The lactate concentration decreased at a faster rate with »active« recovery. Thirty minutes after the cessation of exercise the resting blood lactate level was reached during »active« recovery, whereas the level was more than 10 times higher than at rest after 30 minutes of »passive« recovery.

Recovery activities

A training session or match should end with a period of recovery activities consisting of jogging and stretching exercises.

Jogging

During a match or an intense training session lactate accumulates in the active muscles. Light recovery exercise will help to remove the lactate more quickly. This is illustrated in Fig. WR9, which shows that during low intensity running blood lactate decreases at least three times more rapidly than at rest. The faster removal is one of the reasons as to why a training session or a match should end with low intensity activities such as jogging or a „passive" small-sided game for at least five minutes.

Stretching

Stretching is defined as an exercise where a muscle is fully extended and held in that position for at least 15 seconds. It is important for a soccer player to be flexible, as poor range of movement can hinder performance and cause the muscle to rupture in situations during a match where the muscle is forced into an extreme position.

It has been demonstrated that the length of certain muscles in the legs are considerably shortened following a soccer match, and it can take more than two days before the normal length is restored. Playing matches and training frequently without performing regular stretching can result in a permanent shortening of the muscles. Thus ending a match or training session by stretching the main muscle groups used in soccer will help to restore the length of the muscles.

During shecthing the coach has the opportunity to talk with the player

How to stretch

During a stretch, the two ends of a muscle are drawn away from each other. For example, a quadriceps muscle can be stretched by bending the leg and pressing the heel towards the buttocks while the hip is pressed forward.

There are several ways to perform stretching exercises (for further description see the book „Specific Muscle Training in Soccer"). A simple and efficient method is described below.

Slowly bring the muscle to a fully stretched position and hold this position for 10 seconds, then carefully stretch the muscle some more and hold this position for another 10 seconds.

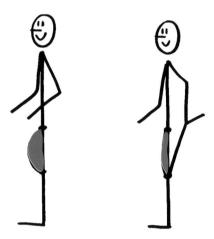

When stretching there are certain rules to observe:

- The muscles must be warm
- Always use slow movements and do not bounce
- Never stretch with a bent back and straight legs
- Be careful when stretching with a partner

Both before and after a muscle is stretched it should be activated. If, for instance, the quadriceps muscles are to be stretched, the player can perform light kicking exercises or jumping before and after the stretching. Such activities also ensure that the muscles stay warm during the entire stretching programme.

A player should not start to stretch immediately after leaving the changing room as the muscles are cold and the risk of injury is high. For the same reason, a player should only perform light stretching exercises during a warm-up. A full stretching programme can be carried out after warm-up and after training.

A stretching programme

The six stretching exercises described below make up a short, but effective stretching programme for a soccer player. Each stretched position should be held for approximately 20 seconds, and activities performed between the stretching exercises should be of equal duration. The whole programme lasts approximately four minutes. If further stretching is desired, alternative exercises can be added or the programme can be repeated.

Calf muscles

Press the heel of the stretched leg towards the ground and keep the hip high.

Quadriceps muscle

Lift the knee, hold the foot with a hand, and press the heel towards the buttocks while pressing the hip forward.

Hamstring muscles

Stretch one leg forward with the toes pointing up. Bend the other leg. The body is held in an almost upright position and the buttock is pressed down. If the opposite arm is stretched forward the buttocks will be pressed further down.

Leg adductor muscles

With one leg bent and pointed forward, stretch the other leg to the side. Both feet are pointing forward and are kept on the ground. Slowly press the buttocks down. The upper body should be almost upright (slightly bent forward). Do not press with the hands on the stretched leg. The knee of the bent leg must be held directly above the foot (no twisting of the knee joint).

Deep abdominal muscles

One leg is bent and placed forward (the knee must not be in front of the ankle). The opposite leg is held back with the leg half bent and with the knee on the ground. The hip of this leg is pushed forward. The hamstring muscles of the leg held in front are partly stretched, while the deep abdominal muscles connected to the leg held in back are fully stretched. By regularly stretching the deep abdominal muscles the risk of getting a groin injury can be reduced; yet this type of exercise is often neglected among soccer players.

Buttock muscles

Cross one leg over the other and press carefully on the knee and thigh of the leg with the opposite arm. The other arm can either rest on the ground or be held behind the back, which makes the exercise more difficult. Keep the upper body erect. To make the exercise easier, the lower leg can be stretched or the other arm can press on the knee.

Muscles should be stretched at the end of a warm-up.

Adaptation to recovery activities
Often players are heading straight for the changing room after a training session and a match. It may take some time before the players become accustomed to recovery activities and accept a change to this routine. The initial programme should therefore be simple and it should be led by the coach, who should frequently reinforce the value of recovery activities. As the players become aware of the positive effects of recovery activities they may perform the exercises on their own.

Summary

Before a match or a training session a player should warm up in order to improve performance and to reduce the risk of becoming injured. The exercises in a warm-up programme should be technically simple and begin at a low intensity and then gradually increase. After a match and a training session a player should perform recovery activities in order to recover as efficiently as possible.

The Training Session

This chapter deals with practical aspects of a training session. It describes heart rate and outlines general principles of why and how to monitor a player's heart rate during training. The chapter also covers a description of how to use and change intensity in a training drill.

What is heart rate?

The function of the heart is to pump blood around the body. Heart rate refers to the number of times the heart beats per minute. In a resting state, heart rate is about 60 beats per minute (beats/min). Well-trained endurance athletes have a lower resting heart rate which, in extreme cases, can be below 30 beats/min. During exercise the heart rate rises in relation to increased intensity. The maximum heart rate for young women and men around 20 years of age is about 200 beats/min. However, there is a large range within a given age group. In a study of a group of boys and girls aged 16 to 19 years, maximum heart rate ranged from 180 to 230 beats/min. Maximum heart rate decreases as age increases. A-20 year old individual with a maximum heart rate of 195 beats/min might have a heart rate of only 175 beats/min when 60 years old.

Training influences heart rate during exercise. Aerobic training causes an increase in the amount of blood that the heart pumps out per heart beat (stroke volume), thus the heart does not have to beat so often in order to pump out the same amount of blood. Therefore, the heart rate will be lower at a given exercise intensity after a period of training (see Fig. TS1, page 78). Training does not, however, affect the maximum heart rate.

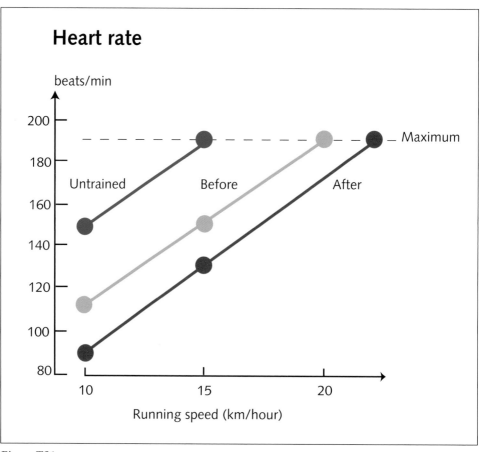

Figure TS1

The figure illustrates how training affects heart rate. Before and after a period of training a player's heart rate was recorded at three different running speeds. After the training, the heart rate was lower for the two lower running speeds, whereas the heart rate was unchanged during the maximal running. For comparison, values for an untrained person with the same maximum heart rate as the player are also shown.

How to measure heart rate

Heart rate can be measured by the pulse from the large artery of the wrist or the neck (see Fig. TS2). The heart rate is expressed as the number of heart beats per minute. The number of beats can be counted for 6, 10, 15, or 30 seconds. To obtain the number of beats per minute these values should be multiplied by 10, 6, 4, or 2, respectively (see example in Scheme TS1). The longer the counting time used, the smaller the measurement error will be. On the other hand, heart rate decreases fairly quickly upon cessation of exercise. To obtain information about heart rate during an exercise period, it is therefore best to use a counting time of 15 seconds immediately after the exercise.

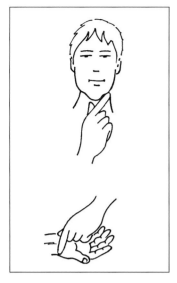

Figure TS2
The figure shows two locations to measure heart rate. One should never press on both sides of the neck

It is important that players can measure their own heart rate as well as that of others. Once the players have learned the technique, heart rate measurements can be performed in a short time. In order to maintain a high training efficiency, it may be advantageous to determine heart rate at the beginning of recovery periods.

The 15-second time period needed to measure heart rate can be controlled by the coach who shouts „3-2-1" and „GO". A stop-watch is started on the command „GO" and the players start counting heart beats. The first beat is counted as zero. After exactly 15 seconds the coach gives a signal for the players to stop counting and the numbers obtained by the players are multiplied by four to give the number of heart beats per minute. The coach may then inform the players of the range in which the heart rate should be. In this way the players will receive feedback as to whether they have exercised at the desired intensity. An alternative to manual heart rate determinations is to use heart rate monitors, which allows continuous measurements and storage of heart rate during the training. Thus, the entire training session can be evaluated afterwards.

Counting time	Multipliction factor	Counted number x Factor	= Heart rate
6 sec	10	16 x 10	= 160 beats/min.
10 sec	6	27 x 6	= 162 beats/min.
15 sec	4	40 x 4	= 160 beats/min.
20 sec	3	54 x 3	= 162 beats/min.

Scheme TS1

Modern telemetric equipment makes it possible to monitor heart rate during training and matches without any inconvenience for the players.

Exercise intensity and heart rate

During exercise the heart rate rises in relation to increased intensity, therefore the heart rate is useful in the evaluation of the intensity of an activity in soccer. The exercise intensity of a player will vary frequently during a game. This is in part dependent on the position of the player in relation to the ball. Nevertheless, to a certain degree the heart rate will reflect the variations in exercise intensity. Figure TS3 shows an example of the fluctuations in heart rate for a player during a seven-a-side game using three-quarters of the field. This demonstrates that the time when heart rate is measured is crucial. The range of heart rates was 102 to 178. One might speculate that the exercise intensity of the player was too low when the heart rate was 102 beats/min, and too high when the heart rate was 178 beats/min. Neither assumption, however, would be correct, as the player's average heart rate was 152 beats/min, which was within the desired range for the game. Thus, to evaluate a player's average exercise intensity during a training game, heart rate measurements should be made on different occasions during the game.

In order to become familiar with heart rate measurements, a player's heart rate can be measured after different activities during a training game, and the values can be compared with those shown in Fig. TS3.

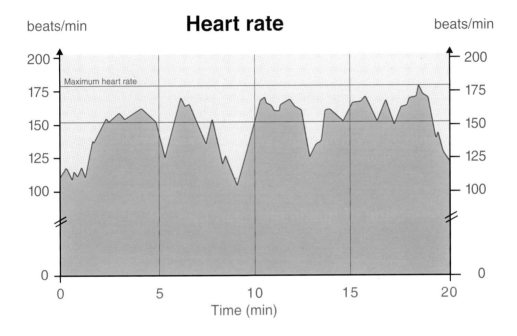

Figure TS3
The figure shows changes in heart rate of a player during a seven-a-side game on half a field. Note the large variations in heart rate. The average heart rate was 152 beats/min.

Reasons for monitoring heart rate

Heart rate determinations can give an indication of how hard a player is working and can be used to evaluate if the aim of a training session is fulfilled. These measurements are especially useful when a player is expected to exercise at a high intensity. Regular monitoring of heart rate during training can also provide a good stimulus for the players to work harder. However, there are certain points that should be considered before using heart rate determinations for training as discussed below.

Maximum heart rate

In order to make optimal use of heart rate measurements during training it is necessary to know the maximum heart rate for each player. For example, a heart rate of 170 beats/min recorded during a training game could reflect a very high exercise intensity for a player with a maximum heart rate of 180 beats/min (exercising at a level corresponding to 94% of maximum heart rate). However, for a player with a maximum heart rate of 230 beats/min the exercise would be less demanding, as 170 beats/min would correspond to only 74% of maximum heart rate.

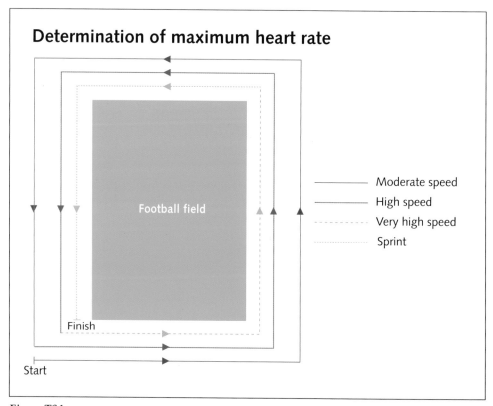

Figure TS4
The figure illustrates a method to determine a player's maximum heart rate.

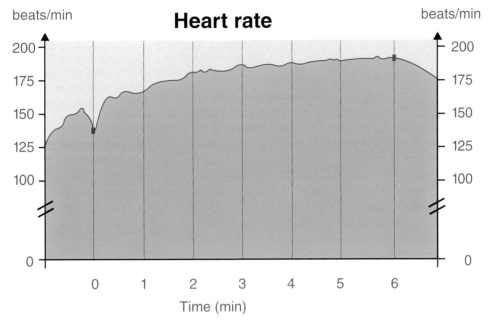

Figure TS5
The figure shows an example of how heart rate change during the maximal heart rate test performed for six minutes after a warming-up period. Note that heart rate increase progressively and reach maximum level before the end of the test.

A player's maximum heart rate can be determined in a simple way, as described below (see Fig. TS4).

The player runs four laps around a soccer field at a moderate speed corresponding to a pace of about two minutes per lap (or another type of warm-up). This is followed by running one lap at a higher speed (in about 90 seconds), then half a lap in about 40 seconds, and finally half a lap at maximal speed, which may take about 30 seconds. Immediately after finishing the test, the player's heart beats are counted for 15 seconds and this number is multiplied by four to give the number of beats per minute. The test lasts around 11 minutes for each player. The duration of the test can be as short as three minutes if another type of warm-up is used. If a whole team is to be tested, the players can start at intervals of 30 seconds, thus, 16 players can be tested (including warm-up) in 20 minutes. Figure TS5 shows an example of how heart rate changed during such a maximal test.

Another way to determine a player's maximum heart rate is to measure it immediately after a bout of presumed maximal intensity exercise during training. However, such measurements should be repeated several times to ensure that the true maximum heart rate has been obtained.

A player's maximum heart rate will not vary with changes in training status throughout the season, but it will decrease as a player gets older. It is therefore only necessary to determine a player's maximum heart rate once a year.

When to monitor heart rate

The coach has many things to do during a training session, such as organising, instructing, and observing, so the additional responsibility of performing heart rate measurements may appear to be an unnecessary burden. However, such measurements can be made infrequently until the players and the coach are well acquainted with the procedures. Initially, the coach may only do heart rate measurements during selected training drills. When the expected range of heart rates for a given drill is known, random checks can be made.

Occasionally, heart rates should also be monitored during games, which are designed to focus on aspects other than fitness. In this way the coach can obtain valuable information about how these games complement the fitness training.

One should be aware that the actual intensity of a game or exercise is influenced by many factors, such as motivation, technical standard of the players, and the condition of the ground. Another aspect is that players often keep a higher activity level than usual if they know that attention is being focused on their efforts.

Training drills

In the following chapters several training exercises and games (referred to as drills) will be presented. The descriptions of the drills are divided into a number of sub-sections, which are described in general terms below.

Area
The approximate dimensions of the playing area used for each drill are described. The actual size is determined by the number of players. The playing area is also illustrated by a diagram in which the area is marked inside a regular soccer field. Whenever possible the original lines of the field are used in order to facilitate preparation.

Number of players
A suggestion for the number of players needed to fulfil the purpose of the drill is given. Variations in the number of players that can be used are indicated in brackets, but this is only a guideline and does not mean that the drill cannot function with more or fewer players. If the number of players is changed, it may be necessary to change the size of the playing area.

Below the different codes for number of players are explained (five is used as an example):

5v5 (ten players in total - two teams of five players) means that five players from one team play against five from another team.

5v5+2 goalkeepers (twelve players in total - two teams of six players) means that five players from one team play against five from another team, each team has a goalkeeper.

5+5v5 (fifteen players in total - three teams of five players) means that ten players from two teams play against five players from a third team.

5+5v5+5 (twenty players in total - two teams of ten players) means that each team consists of two sets of five players that take turns to play. Five players from each team start the game while the other players rest. After a certain time substitutions are made for both teams.

2x5v5 (twenty players in total - two teams of ten players) means that five players from one team play against five players from another team, while at the same time the remaining five players from each team play against each other in another area.

Organisation
The positions of the players at the start of the drill are described. Suggestions are made as to how to progress from one phase of the drill to the next.

Description
The drill is first described in general terms and then in more detail.

Rules
The rules for the drill are described. If nothing else is mentioned the drill is played with normal soccer rules.

Special terms are used for the number of ball touches allowed. A minimum of two touches means that a player has to touch the ball at least twice every time the player gets the ball; a maximum of two touches means that the ball must not be touched more than twice when a player has the ball. Excact two touches means that each player has to touch the ball twice everytime the player gets the ball. If the imposed conditions are broken during a drill, possession is given to the other team. A team gains possession of the ball when the ball is captured and two players from the team then touch it consecutively.

Scoring
A scoring system that can be used for each drill is described. Scoring can be achieved either by scoring a goal as in a normal game or through scoring points. A way in which a final result can be reached is also suggested.

Some form of scoring will often motivate the players. In order to ensure that this effect is sustained throughout the game it is important to keep to the rules of the drill and to count the scores correctly. It is advisable to let the players apply the rules and keep score themselves.

Type of exercise
Exercise can be classified as being either continuous or intermittent. Continuous exercise is performed at a fairly constant intensity for a prolonged period of time. During intermittent exercise the level of intensity changes markedly and can include rest periods. When intermittent exercise is described, suggestions are made for the duration of the exercise and rest periods. These can be varied in several ways within the given limits.

Variations
Variations to the drill are presented. Variations can be introduced simply for a change, or to alter the intensity of the exercise.

Hints for the coach
Suggestions are made as to how to introduce the drill to the players, especially if the drill includes specific conditions. An indication of the expected exercise intensity is also given. The coach should observe whether the actual intensity is as expected.

   If the exercise intensity does not correspond to that desired, the players may not have fully understood the purpose of the drill. The coach should then explain the principles of the game again and elaborate on the possibilities that exist within the drill. Perhaps more time is needed for the players to become accustomed to the game. It may be that the drill does not function well with the particular group of players. In this case the drill should be adjusted, for example, by changing the number of players, the size of the playing area, or the number of ball touches (see page 87). Another possibility is to use the suggestions described within the drill under the section „change of intensity". The probable effect of the described variations is also given.

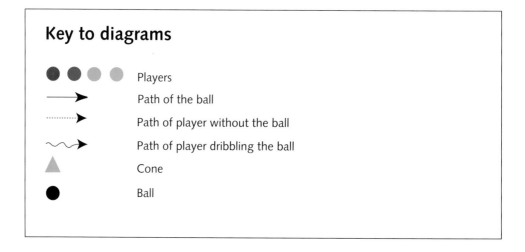

Key to diagrams

●　●　●　●　　Players

──────►　　Path of the ball

┈┈┈┈┈►　　Path of player without the ball

〜〜〜►　　Path of player dribbling the ball

▲　　Cone

●　　Ball

Adjustment circle

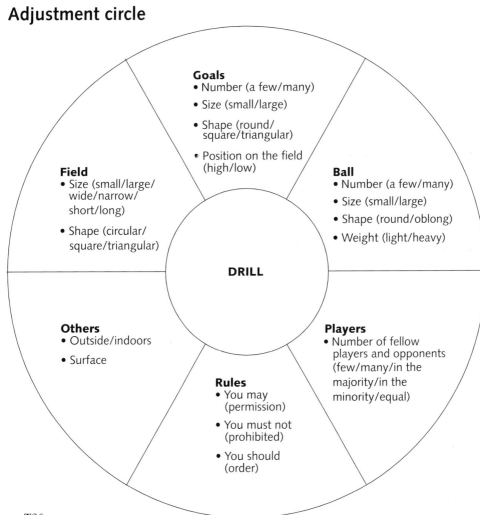

Figure TS6
The figure illustrates the adjustment circle, which describes various areas in which a drill can be altered in order to change the exercise intensity.

Varying a drill
If the purpose of a training drill is not being fulfilled, changes should be made. In fitness training it is mainly the exercise intensity that needs to be controlled. There are many ways in which a drill can be adjusted, and some examples are outlined within the description of the drill. One possibility is to change the rules; e.g. all the players of a team must be in the attacking half of the field before a goal can be scored. The „adjustment circle" (see Fig. TS6) shows various areas where changes can be made and Fig. TS7 (see page 88) illustrates an example of the effect of implementing a suggestion given in

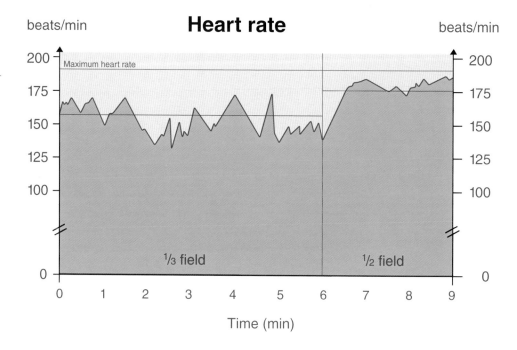

Figure TS7

The figure shows heart rate of a player during a five-a-side game played on one-third of a field. After increasing the playing area to one-half of a field, the average heart rate increased by 14 beats/min. Thus, by implementing a change in the "rules" of the game, the overall work rate of the player increased (see also Fig. TS6).

the adjustment circle. The condition of a maximum of two ball touches was included in a seven-a-side game on half a field and resulted in an increase of the average heart rate from 152 to 163 beats/min.

Summary

Monitoring heart rate can be used to evaluate training effectiveness, but considerations should be made with regards to fluctuations in heart rate within a given drill and to a player's maximum heart rate. General ideas of how to change the intensity of a game have also been provided in this chapter.

Aerobic Training

Aims

- To increase the capacity of the oxygen transporting system.

- To increase the capacity of muscles to utilise oxygen during prolonged periods of exercise.

- To increase the ability to recover rapidly after a period of high-intensity exercise.

Effects

The main physiological adaptations to aerobic training are:

- The blood volume increases and the heart becomes larger and stronger so it can pump more blood per unit of time. More oxygen can then be transported, thus increasing the aerobic energy production during high-intensity exercise.

- The capacity to utilise oxygen and to oxidise fat in the muscle increases. This means that less carbohydrate (glycogen) is used at a given exercise intensity and the limited stores of this fuel are spared.

The benefits for soccer are

- A larger percentage of the energy required for exercise can be supplied aerobically, which means that a player can work at a higher exercise intensity for prolonged periods of time during a match.

- An improved endurance which allows a player to exercise at a higher intensity throughout a game.

- Less time is required to recover after a period of high-intensity exercise before being able to perform maximally in a subsequent match activity.

Aerobic training can also help to minimise deterioration of technical performance and lapses in concentration induced by fatigue, which may occur towards the end of a game.

Types of aerobic training

Aerobic training can be divided into three overlapping areas: aerobic low-intensity training (Aerobic$_{LO}$), aerobic moderate-intensity training (Aerobic$_{MO}$), and aerobic high-intensity training (Aerobic$_{HI}$, see Fig. AE1).

As aerobic training should mainly be performed with a ball, the definition of the three categories of aerobic training takes into account that the heart rate of a player will alternate continuously during training. Scheme AE1 illustrates the principles behind the various categories of aerobic training. It is misleading to quantify training by the total exercise time. Any activity, whether it lasts for 15 or 90 minutes, can have a favourable effect on a player's aerobic work capacity.

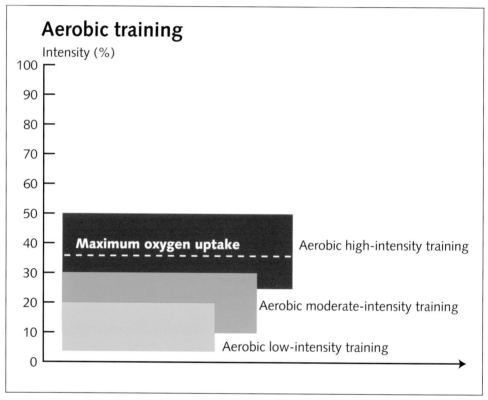

Figure AE1. Components of aerobic training.

	Heart rate			
	% of HR max		Mean* Range* Beats/min.	
	Mean	Range	Mean*	Range*
Low-intensity training	65%	50-80%	130	100-160
Moderate- intensity training	80%	65-90%	160	130-180
High- intensity training	90%	80-100%	180	160-200

Scheme AE1. Principles of aerobic training
*If HR_{max} is 200 beats/min

Aerobic low-intensity (Aerobic$_{LO}$) training

Aim
To achieve faster recovery after a match or an intensive training session.

Application to soccer
During a match or intensive training small ruptures may occur in the connective tissue and fibres of the muscle. This damage, which is often still present several days after it has been induced, causes the muscle to become stiff and hard. Performance is reduced and the ability to replenish glycogen stores is inhibited. The typical symptom that the player experiences is local muscle soreness.

During Aerobic$_{LO}$ training the players perform light physical activities, such as jogging and low intensity games. This type of training can help the muscle recover more efficiently and can reduce muscle soreness. Aerobic$_{LO}$ training can also be used to avoid a condition known as „overtraining" (see also page 196). Throughout the season, when players are training frequently and playing many competitive matches, there may be times when the body is not able to recover completely. In such cases Aerobic$_{LO}$ training should replace more physically demanding forms of training. Due to its function Aerobic$_{LO}$ training is also called recovery training.

Aerobic$_{LO}$ training also has psychological benefits. The need to recover physically is often accompanied by a need to relax mentally. This may be obtained by performing exercises of low intensity and activities that differ from those normally used.

Principle

During Aerobic$_{LO}$ training the exercise intensity should be such that a player's heart rate is:

Average: Approx. 65% of maximal heart rate (HR$_{max}$)
Range: 50%-80% of HR$_{max}$

For a player with a HR$_{max}$ of 190 beats/min this corresponds to:

Average: Approx. 120 beats/min
Range: 95-150 beats/min

The heart rate should not exceed the recommended upper limit for more than a short period of time.

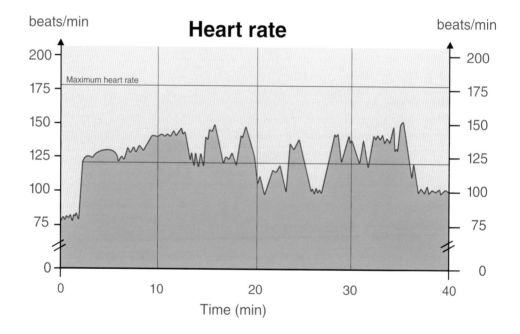

Figure AE2

The figure shows heart rate of a player during a 40-minute period of Aerobic. The average heart rate was 125 beats/min with a range from 100 to 150 beats/min.

Aerobic low intensity training.

The training can take the form of either continuous or intermittent exercise. For the intermittent exercise the work periods should be longer than five minutes. Figure AE2 shows an example of the fluctuations in heart rate for a player during a low-intensity training drill.

Organisation
The need for Aerobic$_{LO}$ training, after a match or intensive training session, will vary from player to player depending on fitness level and how hard the player worked. Some players can comfortably perform harder exercises than those of Aerobic$_{LO}$ training on the day after a match or intense training session. Therefore, the activities to be performed should be selected according to the individual need. In order to elevate the motivation of players, who do not feel like training on the day following a match, it is advisable that the whole squad warms up together.

Aerobic$_{LO}$ training drills

In Aerobic$_{LO}$ training it is good to use drills that do not heavily stress sore muscles and in which physical contact is avoided. Aerobic$_{LO}$ training without a ball can consist of 20-40 minutes of jogging. Two drills for Aerobic$_{LO}$ training with a ball are described below.

Drill 1 – Soccer Croquet (Fig. AE3)

Area: Half a soccer field.

Number of players: 14 (2 to 24).

Organisation: The players are divided into teams of two. Each team starts at any obstacle with a ball. All teams start at the same time.

Description: The players in each team work together and must alternate touching the ball. An obstacle is passed when the ball is played from one player to the other.

Rules: There are three different ways to pass an obstacle:

1. Two cones: the ball is played between the cones.

2. Four cones in the shape of a square: The ball is first played in one direction through the square and then diagonally through the other direction.

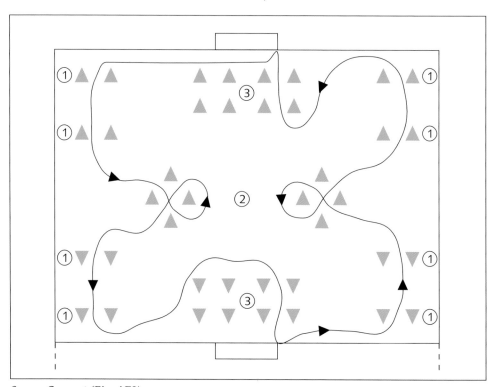

Soccer Croquet (Fig. AE3)

3. Four cones and a post: The ball is played between the cones and onto the post with one touch.

Scoring: The coach sets a lap time for the course. The players must then try to complete each lap in a time which is as close to the set time as possible. The players should not be given any information regarding their lap time during the activity. The winning team is the team that comes closest to keeping the correct tempo. For example, if the coach chooses a lap time of three minutes and stops the drill after nine minutes, the team that has come closest to completing three laps wins the game.

Variations: a. The ball must be kept moving at all times.

b. The players are allowed to touch the ball more than once (free touch) but the ball must be played between the cones with a first touch pass.

c. The number of times the ball can be touched is limited to a maximum of three per player.

d. No set time - the team that uses the least number of touches per lap wins.

Hints for the coach: The coach should demonstrate how to pass the different obstacles. It is important to explain clearly that the scoring system demands a controlled low tempo and that emphasis should not be placed on speed. The players should be allowed a practice lap, during which regular times are given. It is important that the lap time set by the coach necessitates a low tempo. The players should not be told the total duration of the drill or the total number of laps that have to be completed, as this defeats the competitive object of the game.

Change of intensity:
The exercise intensity of the drill should be very low. This is determined by both the lap time and how difficult it is to pass the obstacles. The latter can be varied in several ways, e.g. by changing the distance from the cones to the post.

Drill 2 – Soccer golf (Fig. AE4)

Area: Unlimited area.

Number of players: 6v6 (1v1 -13v13).

Organisation: A number of cones are positioned within the playing
                               area. Each player has a ball. A player from one team
                               competes against a player from the opposing team.

Description: Players should try to hit the cone with as few kicks as
                              possible. After hitting the cone the players continue to
                              the next cone, „teeing off" about five metres from the
                              last cone.

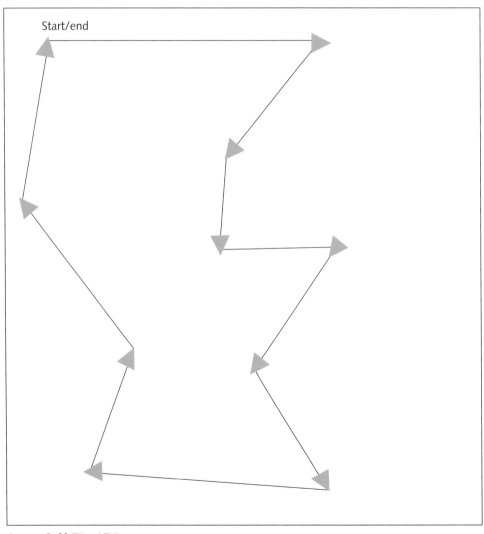

Soccer Golf (Fig. AE4)

Rules:	None.
Scoring:	The player that has used the fewest kicks to hit the cones wins the game and receives two team points. One point is awarded to each team if a game is tied. The team which finishes with the most points wins the game.
Variations:	a. Each team is divided into groups of three players. Each group has one ball. The players in the group have to play the ball every third time. The ball must not stop until it hits the cone.
	b. Match-play golf. The player that needs the fewest kicks to hit a cone gets 1 point (tie = 0 points). If a cone is not hit within 10 kicks the player has to continue to the next cone. The player that has scored the most points at the end wins the game, and this player's team receives two points.
Hints for the coach:	The players should be carefully instructed about the rules and the placement of the cones (including the order of hitting them). The game can be made more entertaining by placing some of the cones in difficult positions, e.g. on a slope or behind a tree.
	Change of intensity: The game should be played with a low exercise intensity. However, the players should not stand still for long periods of time. Variation b. should reduce the duration of the waiting periods. In order to avoid a queue at the beginning of the game, pairs of players can start from different cones.

Aerobic moderate-intensity (Aerobic$_{MO}$) training

Aims

- To increase the capacity to exercise for prolonged periods of time.

- To increase the ability to recover quickly after a period of high-intensity exercise.

Application to soccer

A top-class soccer player covers a distance of approximately 11 kilometres during a soccer match and also performs other energy demanding activities (see page 20). Therefore, it is important for players to have a high endurance capacity. This capacity can be improved through Aerobic$_{MO}$ training and complimented by Aerobic$_{HI}$ training (see page 106). The desired effect is to improve the ability to maintain a high work-rate and good technical performance throughout the game.

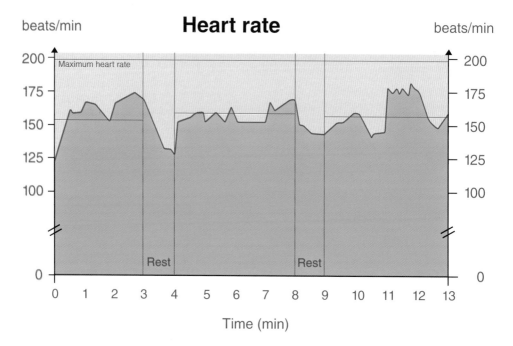

Fig. AE5
The figure shows heart rate of a player during an Aerobic$_{MO}$ game (Scoring Cones, see page 100).

Players during an Aerobic$_{MO}$ game - Chain (see page 104).

Principle

During Aerobic$_{MO}$ training the exercise intensity should be such that a player's heart rate is:

Average:	Approx. 80% of HR$_{MAX}$
Range:	70%-90% of HR$_{MAX}$

For a player with a HR$_{MAX}$ of 190 beats/min this corresponds to:

Average:	Approx. 150 beats/min
Range:	133-170 beats/min

The heart rate should not be below or above the recommended limits for more than a short period of time.

Organisation

Aerobic$_{MO}$ training can take the form of either continuous or intermittent exercise. For the intermittent exercise the work periods should be longer than five minutes. Figure AE5 shows an example of the fluctuations in heart rate for a player during an Aerobic$_{MO}$ training game. If the training is performed without a ball, it is recommended that exercise with varying intensities is used, e.g. alternating between exercise intensities corresponding to 70%, 80%, and 90% of HR$_{MAX}$ each minute.

Aerobic$_{MO}$ training drills

Several games for Aerobic$_{MO}$ training are described below.

Game 1 - Scoring Cones (Fig. AE6)

Area:	Half a soccer field.
Number of players:	5v5 (3v3 - 8v8).
Organisation:	Each team defends a row of cones (five or more). The cones are positioned at least one metre apart in a straight line, in each team's own half of the field.
Description:	With the ball, each team tries to knock over the cones of the opposing team. When a team succeeds, they place the cone back on the opponents' line and, in addition, fetch one of their own cones and place it on the same line. The player who knocks down the original cone must do this task, the other players continue the game. Note: Play is allowed both in front of and behind the line of cones.
Rules:	None.
Scoring:	The game is won by the team which has the fewest cones left after a set time.
Variations:	a. When a player knocks down one of the opponents` cones it should be brought back to the own line of cones. The winning team is then the team, which has the most cones at the end of the game.
	b. The distance between the cones can vary or the cones can stand in small groups.
	c. A cone can only be knocked down by a first time shot.
	d. If a player who is transporting a cone between the two lines is hit by the ball, the cone must be returned.
	e. The cones do not have to be placed on a line. They just have to be positioned somewhere in a team's own half of the field.
	f. The game can be played with two balls.
	g. All the attacking players need to be behind the cones to score a cone (only score from behind).

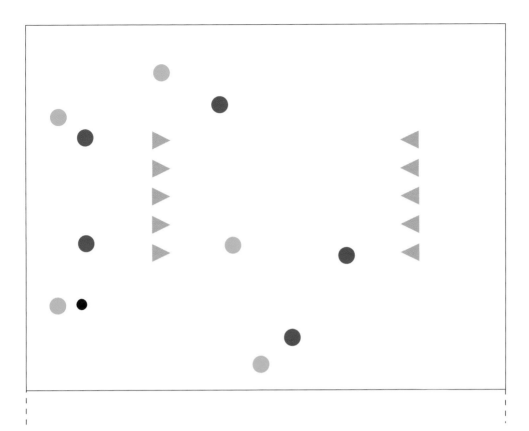

Scoring Cones (Fig. AE6)

Hints for the coach: To prevent the players from working together in small groups, more cones can be added or the distance between the cones can be increased (see variation b. and e.).

Once the players are familiar with the game they can be allowed to position the cones they are attacking or defending. The teams should be encouraged to discuss tactics, e.g. is it best to place the cones in small groups or to spread them out as much as possible? Variation a. can be used to make the game more difficult for the team that is ahead.

Change of intensity:
If the level of intensity is too low, a rule may be introduced so that a cone can only be knocked down when all the players from the attacking team are in the opponent's half of the field. The variations b. to g. should also increase the exercise intensity.

101

Game 2 - Stereo Ball (Fig. AE7)

Area: Half a soccer field.

Number of players: 7v7 (4v4 - 11v11).

Organisation: Each team has one ball.

Description: The teams must keep possession of their own ball and at the same time try to capture the ball from the other team.

Rules: If a team kicks one of the balls out of the playing area, possession is given to the other team (one point is scored - see Scoring).

Scoring: A team gets one point when it has possession of both balls. One ball is then returned to the other team and the play is resumed. The game is won by the team which has scored the most points after a given time period.

Variations: a. The number of consecutive ball touches allowed by each player is limited, e.g. a maximum of three.

b. The number of balls is 3 (or 4 - two per team). A point is scored when three balls are captured.

Hints for the coach: The teams should not divide up into two separate groups with one group of players always trying to capture a ball. This may be avoided by decreasing the size of the playing area or by variation b.

Change of intensity:
The exercise intensity may be increased with variation a. and b.

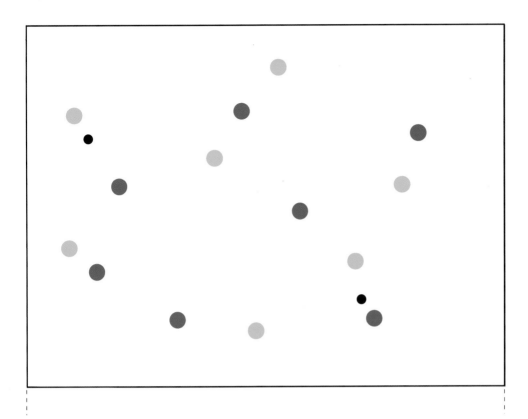

Stereo Ball (Fig. AE7)

Game 3 - Chain (Fig. AE8)

Area:	Three-quarter of a soccer field divided into four zones with two full-size goals.
Number of players:	7v7 (3v3 - 11v11) + 2 goalkeepers.
Description:	Ordinary soccer play.
Rules:	All the players from one team, except the goalkeeper, must be in two adjoining zones.
Variations:	a. The number of passes within a team are limited inside a zone, e.g. a maximum of seven passes the ball has to be played into a new zone.
	b. Each team is allowed to be in three zones instead of two.
	c. The players are no longer required to be in adjoining zones, instead the players from the attacking team (except the goalkeeper) must be inside the opponents´ half of the field before a goal can be scored. All the defending players must also be in this zone. If they are not and a goal is scored, the score is doubled.
Hints for the coach:	Start by explaining the rules of the two adjoining zones. In the transition from one zone to another, all the players from a team must be inside one zone. If this is too difficult fewer players can be used or variation b. can be applied.
	Change of intensity: Increasing the number of zones will often result in a decrease in the exercise intensity. Variation a. should increase the intensity, while b. and c may lower it.

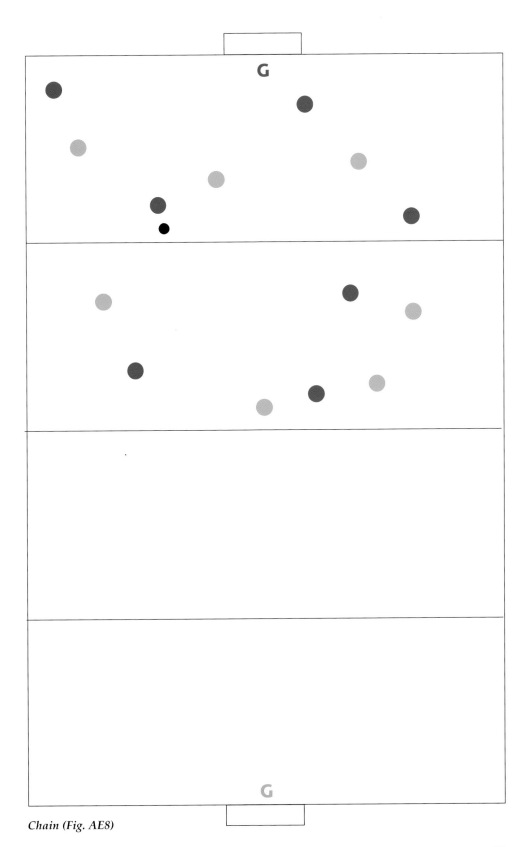

Chain (Fig. AE8)

Aerobic high-intensity (Aerobic$_{HI}$) training

Aims
- To increase the ability to exercise at a high intensity for long periods of time.

- To increase the ability to recover quickly from high-intensity exercise.

Application to soccer
It has been demonstrated that the total distance covered by high-intensity exercise during a match is related to the standard of soccer, i.e. top-class players cover the most distance (see Fig. AE9). Therefore, it is important that players are capable of exercising at high intensities for prolonged periods of time. The basis for this ability is a well-developed capacity to perform aerobic exercise (high maximum oxygen uptake), which can be attained by Aerobic$_{HI}$ training.

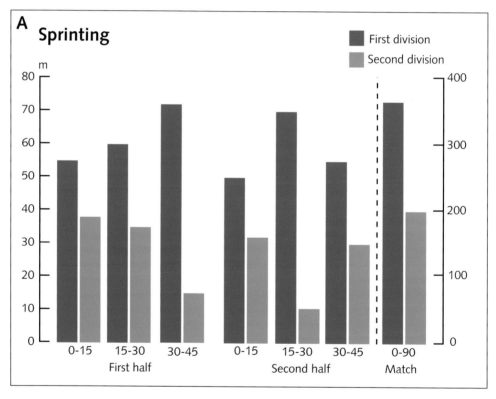

Figure AE9

The figure shows the distance covered by Danish first and second division players during a match within the three categories of high-intensity running. To the left each half of the game has been divided into 15-minute intervals (0-15, 15-30, 30-45 min), and to the right the values for the entire match are given (0-90 min). The first division players performed considerably more high-intensity running than those from the second division.

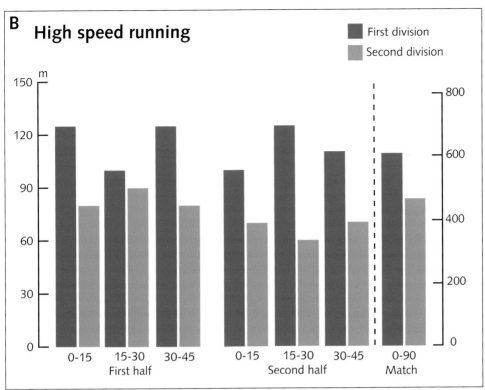

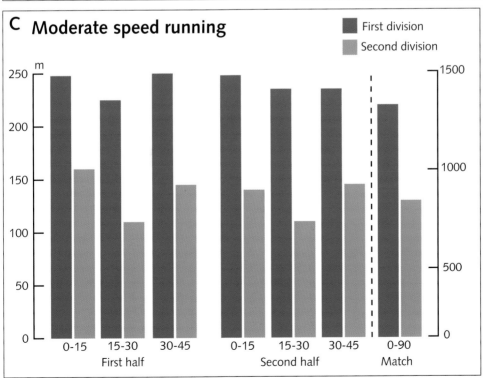

107

Principle

During Aerobic$_{HI}$ training the exercise intensity should be such that a player's heart rate is:

Average: Approx. 90% of HR$_{MAX}$
Range: 80%-100% of HR$_{MAX}$

For a player with a HR$_{MAX}$ of 190 beats/min this corresponds to:

Average: Approx. 170 beats/min
Range: 150-190 beats/min

The heart rate should not be below the recommended lower limit for more than a short period of time.

Overlap with anaerobic speed endurance training

During Aerobic$_{HI}$ training the lactate producing energy system may also be highly stimulated for short periods of time (see Fig. CF10, page 26) which means that the training overlaps anaerobic speed endurance training. The coach should ensure that the exercise intensity during Aerobic$_{HI}$ training does not become so high that the training becomes exclusively speed endurance training. If the intensity is too high, the players will not be able to keep a high enough work rate during subsequent work periods and the desired effect of the Aerobic$_{HI}$ training will be lost.

Organisation

When using games for Aerobic$_{HI}$ training the exercise intensity for a player varies continuously, but a decrease in intensity for a short period of time will only cause a minor decrease in heart rate. Therefore, it is possible for a player to maintain a heart rate above 80% of maximum heart rate for the majority of the training. In addition to the intermittent exercise inherent to soccer, different intermittent training forms can be used in Aerobic$_{HI}$ training. Three of these forms (which to some extent overlap) are described below.

I. Fixed time intervals

The principle of the fixed time intervals is that the duration of the exercise and rest periods is set. If the exercise periods are longer than one minute, the rest periods should be shorter than the exercise periods, otherwise the overall exercise intensity will be too low. Some examples of paired work and rest periods are given in Scheme AE2.

The shorter the exercise periods, the higher the exercise intensity should be (according to the principles given for Aerobic$_{HI}$ training). Rest periods should include some form of recovery exercises, e.g. jogging.

The first intervals shown in Scheme AE2 should not be confused with the similar intervals used in anaerobic speed endurance training, as described on page 153. There is a notable difference in the exercise intensity. During speed endurance training the intensity should be very high for

	Exercise	Rest	Heart rate (% HRmax) (end exercise)
a	1 min	30 sec	90-100%
b	2 min	1 min	85-95%
c	4 min	1 min	80-90%

Scheme AE2. Examples of different exercise and rest periods in Aerobic$_{HI}$

Players during an Aerobic$_{HI}$ game "Back to Back" (see page 128).

the entire exercise period, while it should be considerably lower during Aerobic$_{HI}$ training.

Figure AE10A shows the fluctuations in heart rate of a player during an Aerobic$_{HI}$ training game with exercise periods of two minutes and rest periods of one minute.

The 15/15-principle

In a study, the effect of training by repeatedly alternating 15 seconds of running on a treadmill and 15 seconds of rest was investigated. This form of training is referred to as the 15/15-principle. During the training the aerobic energy system was taxed almost maximally, and the training was shown to improve the subjects´ maximum oxygen uptake. Based on these findings the 15/15-principle is now commonly used in soccer training. However, such short exercise and rest periods are not effective in soccer training drills in which tactical aspects prevent a player from constantly performing aerobic high-intensity exercise, e.g. sometimes it can be tactically more correct for a player to jog than to perform high-intensity exercise. For example, during a three-a-side game on a third of the field, with full-size goals and two

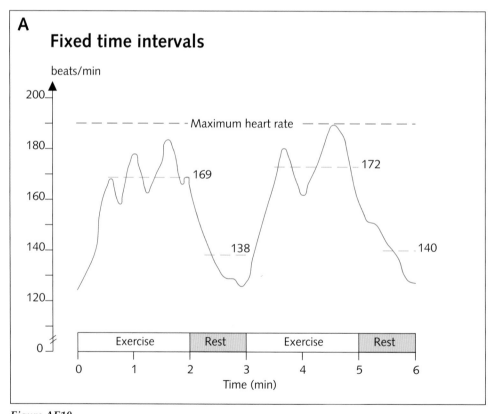

Figure AE10
The figure shows heart rate of a player during Aerobic$_{HI}$ games based upon three different principles: A) Fixed time intervals, B) Alleration of the rules, and C) Natural variations.

B

Change of rules

beats/min

C

Natural variations

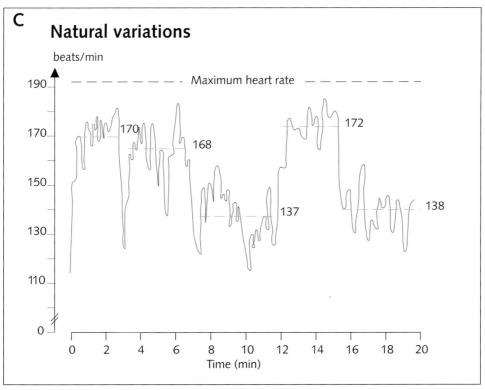

beats/min

Players performing Aerobic$_{HI}$ training – Deep (see page 114).

goalkeepers, there will always be short periods of exercise at a low intensity such as when a goal is scored or when the ball is kicked out of play. These pauses will greatly influence the average exercise intensity if the players are substituted every 15 seconds. Furthermore, a game of this kind can be frustrating as some players rarely get to touch the ball during an exercise period. When using games for Aerobic$_{HI}$ training the duration of the exercise periods should be at least 30 seconds. The use of the 15/15-principle in soccer illustrates that information from scientific research studies should be carefully evaluated before it is applied to soccer training.

II. Alteration of the rules
By changing the rules during a training game the exercise intensity may be varied. Set times can be implemented where the rules are changed to either increase or decrease the intensity. Figure AE10B shows an example of fluctuations in the heart rate of a player during an Aerobic$_{HI}$ training game where the rules have been altered.

III. Natural variations
Training games can be structured so that the exercise intensity changes in a natural way. Figure AE10C shows an example of the fluctuations of a player's heart rate during an Aerobic$_{HI}$ training game where the changes in intensity occurred due to natural variations.

Aerobic$_{HI}$ training drills

Games for the three intermittent training principles within Aerobic$_{HI}$ are described below. Some examples of training without the ball are also given.

Intermittent principle I – Fixed time intervals

Game 1 - Deep (Fig. AE11)

Area:
Approximately one third of a soccer field. The playing area is divided into three zones - two outer-zones (①+③) and a middle-zone (②). The two outer-zones have the same dimensions as the penalty area.

Number of players:
5v5 (3v3 - 10v10).

Organisation:
All players start in the same zone (one of the outer-zones).

Description:
The players can pass the ball within the outer-zones and across the middle-zone, but the ball must not be touched in the middle-zone.

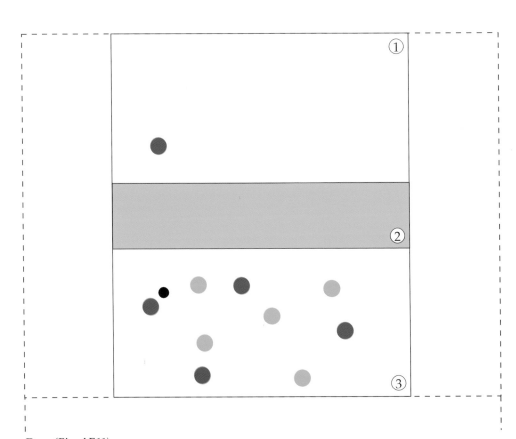

Deep (Fig. AE11)

Rules:	Only one player, from the team in possession of the ball, can be inside the outer-zone opposite to where the ball is. When the ball is played from one outer-zone to the other the players have to change zones before they are allowed to touch the ball.
Scoring:	A team scores a point every second time the ball is played across from one outer-zone to the other and possession is maintained.
Type of exercise:	Intermittent. Fixed time intervals, e.g. exercise periods of three minutes and rest periods of one minute.
Variations:	a. A point is scored if a team can make ten successive passes. The rule of changing zones still applies.
	b. A certain number of passes must be made, e.g. five, within an outer-zone before the ball can be played from one outer-zone to the other.
	c. The ball has to played to the other outer-zone within 8 passes.
	d. The number of ball touches per player is limited, e.g. a maximum of three.
Hints for the coach:	An important component of the game is the shift between zones. As soon as the ball has been played across the middle-zone the players should quickly change zones (high-speed running). During the play in the outer-zones the exercise intensity should also be fairly high, particularly for the defending team.

If variation a. is introduced the coach should emphasise the value of using both outer-zones, as the average exercise intensity of the game may be too low if the players have a tendency to stay inside one zone.

Change of intensity:
By varying the width of the middle-zone, the duration of the high-speed running between the outer-zones can be changed. Variation b. may lower the average exercise intensity while c. and d. should increase it.

Game 2 - Storage (Fig. AE12)

Area: Half a soccer field with four separate zones (1-4).

Number of players: 5v5 (3v3 - 8v8).

Organisation: At least eight balls should be used, equally distri-
                               buted in the four zones. Each team defends and
                               attacks two zones (① + ③ and ② + ④). All players
                               start outside the zones.

Description: The players must take balls from their own zones and
                               try to dribble them into the zones of their opponents.
                               If an opponent touches a ball, the player has to
                               dribble it back to the zone it came from before another
                               attack can be made.

Rules: No player can be attacked while inside a zone. Each
                               team can only have two balls in play at a time.

Scoring: The team that has the most balls in the opponents'
                               zones after a set game-time wins the game.

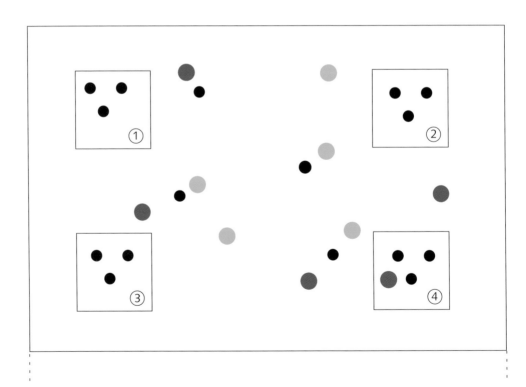

Storage (Fig. AE12)

Type of exercise:	Intermittent. Fixed time intervals, e.g. exercise periods of four minutes and rest periods of one minute.
Variations:	a. A team gains possession of a ball when capturing it.
	b. There is no limit to the number of balls in play at a time.
	c. The players are allowed to pass the ball to each other, so that the player starting with the ball does not necessarily have to dribble it to one of the opponents´ zones.
	d. The two zones which a team is attacking and defending are placed diagonally (① + ④ and ② + ③).
	e. The number of zones can be increased.
Hints for the coach:	The exercise intensity will be the highest for a player who is dribbling the ball towards the opponents´ zone, and for a defending player who is applying pressure to a player with a ball. Variation b. and c. may increase the overall intensity and should be introduced once the players understand the idea of the game.

Change of intensity:
An increase in the number (variation e.) and size of the zones makes it easier to score and should increase the overall exercise intensity. Variation a. may also increase the intensity. |

Game 3 - Shift (Fig. AE13)

Area: About 2/5 of a soccer field with two large goals.

Number of players: 4v4 + 4v4 (2v2 - 6v6) + 2 goalkeepers.

Organisation: Four players from each team are on the field at a time. The other players are positioned as two on each side of own goal. All players are shifted at a given time after a signal from the coach, e.g. „shift". A number of extra balls should be placed on the sides of each goal; so that the goalkeeper easily can get a ball.

Description: Normal play. When the ball passes the sideline or the goal line, the goalkeeper of the team that gets position of the ball starts a „new" ball.

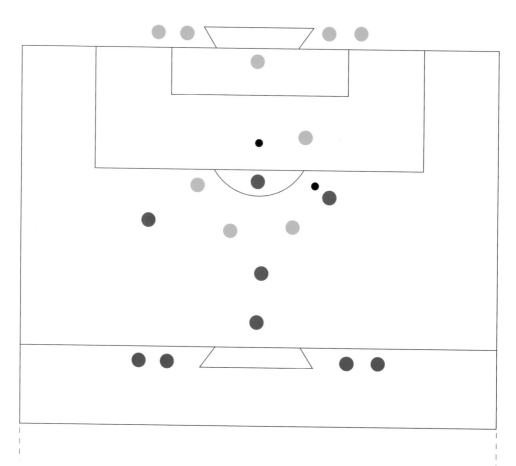

Shift (Fig. AE13)

Rules:	When shifting, none of the players to be shifted must touch the ball (otherwise the opponent will get the ball).
Scoring:	Normal scoring.
Type of exercise:	Fixed time intervals, e.g. 1.5 min of exercise and 1.5 min of rest (while the other part of the team is playing).
Variations:	a. A midline of the field is introduced. All the players need to be in the offensive half for the team to score and the defending team must be on their half, otherwise the scoring counts double.
	b. Each player has a maximum of three touches and the team has a maximum of five passes within the team before they have to shoot on the goal.
	c. Each team has two times two defensive and two offensive players. The defensive players are shifting at own goal line whereas the offensive players are shifting at the opponents` goal line.
	d. When shifting the player that reaches the ball first has to make one pass before the team can score a goal.
Hints for the coach:	The players should be told to exercise with a high intensity when they are on the field. It is a game that involves a high number of shots and it should be emphasised that the goalkeepers have to be very active, not only to save the ball, but also to get the game started rapidly when the ball is out of play. When shifting, the players at the field have to leave the ball and run out of the field at a high speed. In the rest periods, the players should be active, e.g. by jogging to get the balls that pass the goal.

Change of intensity:
Variation a. and b. can be introduced if the overall intensity is too low and variation b. can also be utilised if there are too few shots on goal. Variation c. can be used if the coach wants to make the game more specific for the players' position in the team. Variation d. can be utilised if the players too often shoot immediately after they come into the field.

Game 4 - Goals Galore (Fig. AE14)

Area:	About 1/5 of a soccer field with six small goals.
Number of players:	5:5 (3:3 - 7:7).
Organisation:	Extra balls are positioned in the corners of the field.
Description:	The players must try to dribble through one of the goals (can be done from both sides). If the ball is out of the field, a new ball is taken from one of the corners by the team that gains it.
Rules:	The players are not allowed to run through the goals except when dribbling. After scoring in one goal the team can not score in the same goal immediately after.

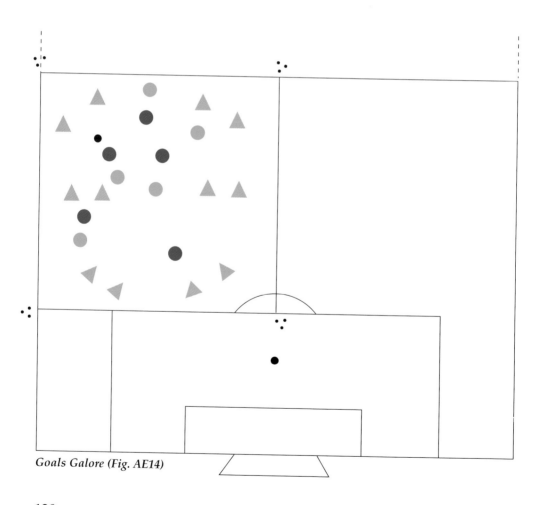

Goals Galore (Fig. AE14)

Scoring:	A point is scored if a player is dribbling through one of the goals.
Type of exercise:	Fixed time intervals, e.g. 3 min of exercise and 1 min of rest.
Variations:	a. A point can only be scored if the ball is passed through one of the goals to a team-mate on the other side of the goal.
	b. Variation a. and scoring is only allowed if the receiving player makes a first time pass to a team-mate and the pass does not go through the goal.
	c. Variation a. and man-to-man marking.
Hints for the coach:	The exercise demands can be controlled by changing both the number and the width of the goals as well as the distance between the goals. The more goals, the wider the goals and the further the goals are positioned from each other, the higher the intensity.
	Change of intensity: Variation a. and b. should increase the overall exercise intensity since more players have to be active in order to score a goal. When introducing variation c., the exercise period should be reduced, e.g. 2 min and 1 min rest. There is a risk that the exercise intensity in this case becomes so high that it becomes speed endurance training (se also page 108).

Intermittent principle II – Altering the rules

Game 1 - Pendulum (Fig. AE15)

Area:	Half a soccer field with two outer-zones (①+③) and a large middle-zone (②).
Number of players:	6v6 (4v4 - 10v10).
Organisation:	One player („outer-player") is positioned in each of the outer-zones whereas the other players are in the middle-zone.
Description:	The teams must transfer the ball from one „outer-player" to the other.
Rules:	An „outer-player" has a maximum of two touches to pass the ball to a player from the team that it was received from. If the „outer-player" touches the ball more than twice or if the ball is played out of the playing area, the other team gets possession of the ball.
Scoring:	A point is scored if a team can transfer the ball from one „outer-player" to the other and then back to the first „outer-player" without the ball being captured by the opposing team. After scoring a point the team can continue and immediately score another point by transferring the ball to the opposite „outer-player".
Type of exercise:	Intermittent. By alternating (e.g. each three minutes) between the ordinary game and variation d. or e. (see below) the overall exercise intensity can be varied.
Variations:	a. The number of times a player can consecutively touch the ball is limited, e.g. a maximum of three.
	b. The „outer-players" are only allowed one touch to play the ball, or the ball must not stop in the outer-zones.
	c. The teams have one „outer-player" in each outer-zone. The players have to pass the ball to an „outer-player" from their own team. The „outer-players" are allowed an unlimited number of ball touches.
	d. Man-to-man marking.

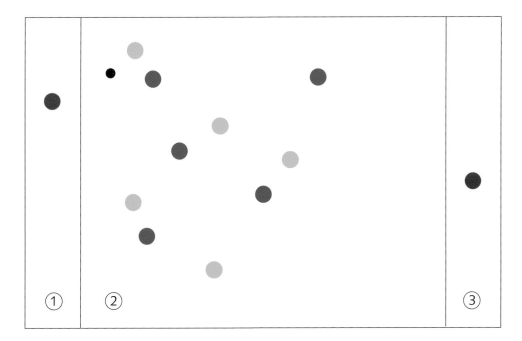

Pendulum (Fig. AE15)

e. All the players on the team in possession of the ball must be on the attacking half of the playing area when the ball is played to the „outer-player".

f. There are no „outer-players" and the size of the outer-zones is extended. A point is scored if a team brings the ball from one outer-zone to the other and returns it to the first zone without the ball being captured by the opposing team. All the players from the team must have been in all „three" outer-zones. The players on the team that is in possession of the ball are not allowed to touch the ball before they have been in the same outer-zone as the ball.

g. Goalkeepers are used as „outer-players" and they may use their hands, but may only hold the ball for 5 seconds.

Hints for the coach:
The players should be encouraged to pass to an „outer-player" as soon as they have captured the ball, and it should be emphasised that it is important to offer support to the „outer-players" after they have received the ball.

Change of intensity:
The exercise intensity can be controlled by varying the number of players and the size of the middle-zone. Variation a., b., d., e. and f. may increase the overall intensity. Variation d. and e. can be useful if some players always stay close to one of the outer-zones.

Intermittent principle III – Natural variations

Game 1 - Position (Fig. AE16)

Area:	Half a soccer field, divided into three adjoining zones with two full-size goals at each end.
Number of players:	6v6 (4v4 - 9v9) + two goalkeepers.
Organisation:	Two players from each team are positioned in the three zones. After a set time the players change zones by rotating (see Fig. AE16): The players from the defending zone move into the middle zone; the players from this zone move into the attacking zone; and the players from the attacking zone move into the defending zone.
Description:	Ordinary soccer play.
Rules:	The players have to stay within their own zones.
Scoring:	Ordinary scoring.

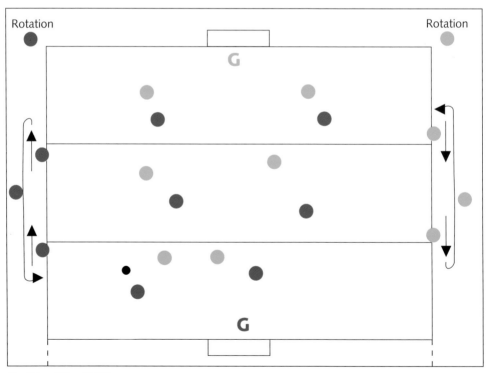

Position (Fig. AE16)

Type of exercise:	Intermittent. For example, exercise periods of four minutes, separated by 30 seconds of rest during which the players change zones.
Variations:	a. Man-to-man marking.
	b. A conditioned number of ball touches, e.g. a minimum of three.
	c. Both players inside a zone must touch the ball before it can be passed into another zone.
	d. The ball must be touched in the middle zone before it can be played into the attacking zone.
	e. The players assigned to the middle zone are allowed to move into the two other zones.
	f. The players assigned to the defending/offensive zone are allowed to move into the middle zone.
	g. When a goal is scored, the direction of the attack is changed.
Hints for the coach:	The players should work intensely when the ball is in their zone. When the ball is in the other zones, they should either defend against an opponent or create space for themselves in order to receive a pass. The game may be most intensive for the players in the middle zone. The changing of zones by rotation should ensure an equal overall exercise intensity for all players.

Change of intensity:
By changing the length and width of the zones the exercise intensity can be altered. Variation a. may be used to increase the work-rate but the intensity should not become so high that the training becomes anaerobic speed endurance training. Variation b. and c. should increase the duration of both the high-intensity exercise periods and the „rest periods". Variation d. will ensure that the players in the middle zone are kept active, and variation e. increase the physical demands placed on these players. Similary, variation will f. increase the average intensity of the other players.

Game 2 - Pressing (Fig. AE17)

Area: A quarter of a soccer field.

Number of players: 5+5v5 (4+4v4 - 6+6v6).

Description: Two teams of five players play against one team of five players. The defending team must try to touch the ball. When the ball is touched the team that lost the ball becomes the defending team.

Rules: None.

Scoring: No points or goals are awarded in this game but if the defending team fails to touch the ball after a set number of passes, e.g. 10, this team has to touch the ball twice before it becomes an attacking team.

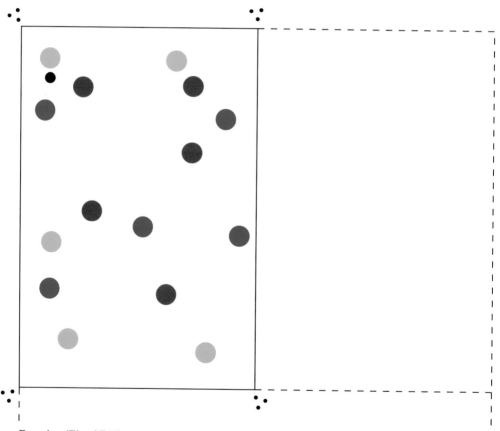

Pressing (Fig. AE17)

Type of exercise:	Intermittent. Natural variations.
Variations:	a. The defending team must gain possession of the ball in order to change with one of the other teams (to become one of the attacking teams).
	b. The ball may not be passed to a player from the same team, i.e. the ball has to alternate between the two attacking teams.
	c. Each player has a conditioned number of ball touches, e.g. a maximum of two.
	d. The players can move to the other quarter of the field and all players have to move.
Hints for the coach:	It is important that the defending team maintains a high exercise intensity. Players of the two teams in possession of the ball should be encouraged to create space and to concentrate on good passing in order to keep the defending team working. The game should be re-started with another ball (placed in the corners) immediately after the defending team has touched the ball so that pauses are minimised.

Change of intensity:
Variation a. will increase the demands of the defending team while b. should increase the exercise intensity of the players that are trying to keep possession of the ball. Variation c. can be used to help the defending team to touch the ball, which may increase the overall exercise intensity. Variation d. may increase the exercise intensity particular for the players with the ball.

Game 3 - Back to Back (Fig. AE18)

Area:	A soccer field divided into three zones - two outer-zones (① + ③) and one middle-zone (②). One goal is placed in the middle of each half. The goals are placed back-to-back.
Number of players:	7v7 (5v5 - 9v9) + 2 goalkeepers.
Description:	Ordinary soccer play.
Rules:	In the middle-zone the number of ball touches is limited to a maximum of two. The goalkeepers may use their hands inside a circular area.
Scoring:	Ordinary scoring.
Type of exercise:	Intermittent. Natural variations.
Variations:	a. Within the middle-zone the number of ball touches per team is limited to a maximum of six. Alternatively, the team can only have three passes in the middle-zone.
	b. In the outer-zones the number of ball touches per player is conditioned, e.g. a maximum of two touches, but free play is allowed in the middle-zone.
	c. All players from the attacking team must be in the same outer-zone before a goal can be scored. If not all of the defending players are within the outer-zone when a goal is scored then the score is doubled.
	d. When the ball is played out of an outer-zone by the attacking team, the goalkeeper starts with a new ball and has to throw it over the middle line.
Hints for the coach:	The exercise intensity should be the greatest when the teams play in the middle-zone.
	Change of intensity: By increasing the length of the middle-zone the physical demands can be elevated. Variation a., c. and d. should increase the average exercise intensity. Variation b. can be used if the teams are too long in the outer-zones.

128

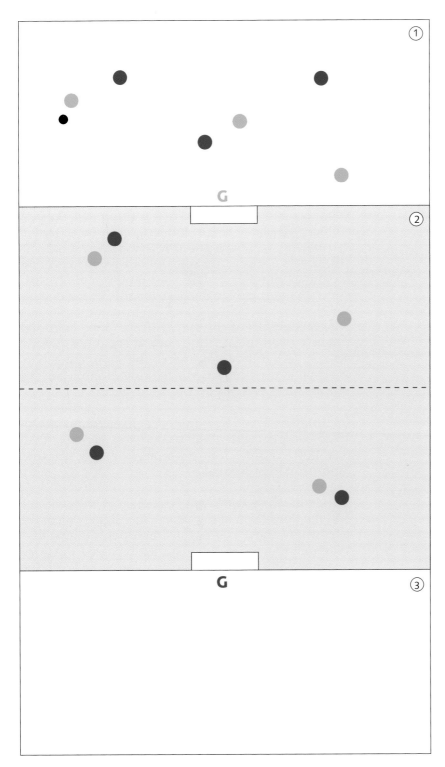

Back to Back (Fig. AE18)

Aerobic_{HI} training without a ball

Exercise 1 – Group Run (Fig. AE19)

Area:	A soccer field or a similar area.
Number of players:	The whole squad.
Organisation:	Two lines are marked approximately five meters away from each side of one of the goal-lines. The players are divided into three groups based on their running ability. The players in the group with the best runners (●) have to run the longest distance (about 110 meters), while the group with the poorest runners (●) covers a shorter distance (about 100 meters), and the remaining players (●) start on the goal-line and cover an intermediate distance (about 105 meters).
Description:	All players start at the end with the three lines and run at a given speed to the opposite goal-line. After a set rest period they run back to the starting position. A signal is used (e.g. a whistle) to indicate when the players have to reach the opposite line.
Type of exercise:	Intermittent. Fixed time intervals. Exercise periods of 15-25 seconds with 15-25-second rest periods. Total duration could, for example, be 20 minutes (approximately 30 runs).
Variation:	Two of the three teams are positioned at one goal-line and the third team at the other. On a signal one of the two teams starts running to the opposite goal-line. When all players in the team have passed the goal-line in the other end, the team waiting at the line starts running to the opposite goal-line, and so on. The running time should be different for the three groups.
Hints for the coach:	The selected running time should be such that the players keep a high speed but are able to maintain the speed for all the exercise periods. Separating the group into three teams should ensure that the relative exercise intensity for each player does not vary too much. If there is an extreme difference in fitness level between players, the distances between the goal-line and the two lines can be extended (e.g. 10 meters), or the players can be divided into more groups (in which case more lines should be added).

Group Run (Fig. AE19)

Exercise 2 – Star Run (Fig. AE20)

Area:	A soccer field or a similar area.
Number of players:	6v6 (2v2 - 12v12).
Organisation:	Cones are placed in the two outer corners of each penalty area, and at the points where the half-way line crosses the side-lines. The players are divided into two teams which should be matched to have equal running abilities.
Description:	Three players run from each team with a dispatch, e.g. a vest. On a given signal these players start running from the edge of the centre-circle to different cones and back to the centre-circle. Thereafter, they run clockwise to the next cone and continue until all six cones have been visited. The dispatch is then given to a team-mate who performs the same course. This continues until a set number of rounds have been completed, e.g. five rounds per player.
Type of exercise:	Intermittent. Exercise periods (one round) of approximately two minutes with two-minute rest periods. Total duration could be 20 minutes (five rounds).
Rules:	The player has to turn around the cones but it is enough just to touch the perimeter of the centre-circle before continuing to the next cone.
Scoring:	The team that first completes the set number of rounds wins.
Variation:	After running to a cone and back to the centre-circle the dispatch is given to a team-mate who runs to the next cone and back to the centre-circle. The dispatch is then given back to the first player who continues to the next cone, and so on.
Hints for the coach:	The players should maintain a high speed around the whole course and they should not sprint at the end of each run, as sprinting may lower the exercise intensity in the subsequent exercise periods.

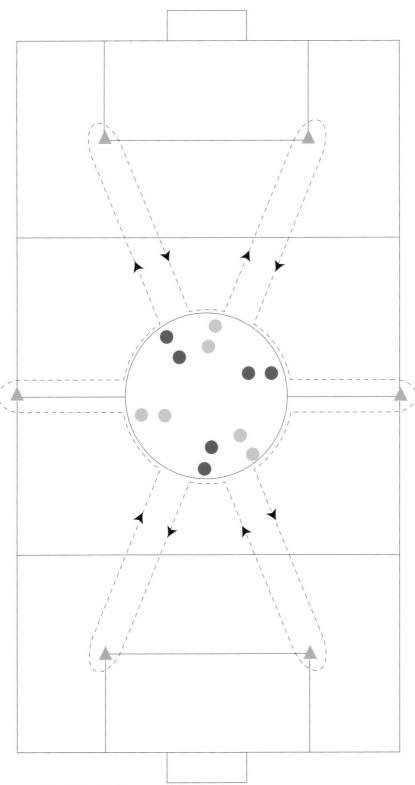

Star Run (Fig. AE20)

Exercise 3 – Pair Running (Fig. AE21)

Area: An area of about 5 x 50 meters.

Number of players: Unlimited number of pairs.

Organisation: The players are divided into pairs consisting of one good and one not so good runner.

Description: On a signal a player from each pair starts running clockwise around the area with a dispatch, e.g. a vest. The other player from each pair walks or jogs around the running area. The players change roles by exchanging the dispatch.

Scoring: The pair completing the most rounds in a set time wins. Only the distance covered by the player with the dispatch counts.

Type of exercise: Intermittent. Exercise periods of 20-120 seconds with 20-120 second rest periods. The total duration could, for example, be 35 minutes, consisting of six periods of five minutes duration separated by one-minute breaks.

Variations: a. The players have to run a minimum of two and a maximum of four rounds during each work bout.

                           b. Each player has to cover five rounds at the first run, then 4, 3, 2, 1, 2, 3, 4, and finish with five rounds.

Hints for the coach: It should be emphasised that the players must not sprint. To obtain a high degree of competition, it is important that the pairs are equally matched. The players who are not running should walk or jog on the outer part of the test area so that they do not obstruct the „high intensity" runners. It might be necessary to introduce variation a. or b. if the good runner covers too many rounds in a row, and the team-mate consequently runs much less.

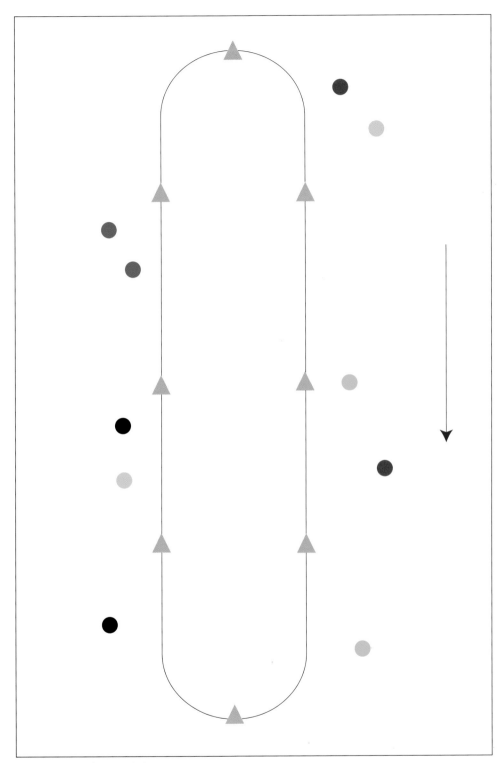

Pair Running (Fig. AE21)

Summary

Aerobic work capacity is a fundamental component of fitness for a soccer player and can be improved by aerobic training. Aerobic training can be divided into three main areas. $Aerobic_{LO}$ training, which aims at helping a player return to pre-exercise status as quickly as possible after a match or a hard training sessions. $Aerobic_{MO}$ training which enables the player to work with a relatively high exercise intensity throughout a match, and $Aerobic_{HI}$ training, which enhances the ability to repeatedly exercise at a high-intensity during a match. In order to obtain the appropriate training effects, the guidelines within the different types of training should be followed (see Scheme AE1, page 91).

Although the training drills described are classified as either $Aerobic_{MO}$ or $Aerobic_{HI}$, many of them can be adapted and used for both types of training simply by changing a rule or the size of the playing area and/or the number of players.

Anaerobic Training

Aims

- To increase the ability to act quickly and to rapidly produce power during high-intensity exercise.

- To increase the capacity to continuously produce power and energy through the anaerobic systems.

- To increase the ability to recover rapidly after a period of high-intensity exercise.

Effects

The main physiological adaptations to anaerobic training are:

- The synchronisation between the nervous system and the muscles becomes more efficient.

- The amount of muscle enzymes involved in anaerobic energy production increases.

- The capacity to produce and remove lactate is elevated.

The benefits for soccer are:

- An improved performance of intense match activities, such as accelerating, sprinting, tackling, and shooting.

- An elevated ability to perform prolonged high-intensity exercise during a game.

- High-intensity exercise can be performed more frequently during a game.

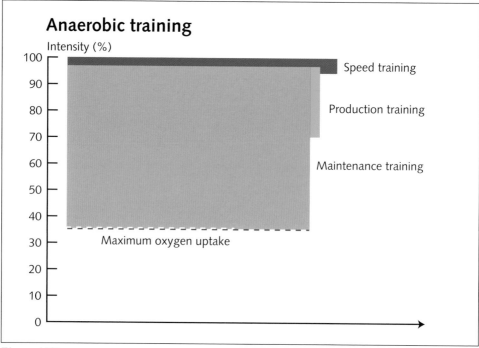

Figure AN1
Components of anaerobic training in soccer.

Types of anaerobic training

Anaerobic training can be divided into speed training and speed endurance training which can be divided into maintenance and production training (see Fig. AN1).

Speed training

Aims

● To increase the ability to perceive match situations that require immediate action (perceiving).

● To increase the ability to take immediate action when needed (evaluating and deciding).

● To increase the ability to rapidly produce force during high-intensity exercise (taking action).

138

	Exercise (s)	Rest (s)	Intensity	No. of repetitions
a	2-5	> 50	Maximal (100%)	5-20
b	5-10	>100	Maximal (100%)	2-10

Scheme AN1. Principles of speed training.

Application to soccer

During a match a player performs many activities that require rapid development of force, such as sprinting or making quick changes in direction. As these activities may influence the outcome of a game, speed training is very important.

Principle

During speed training the players should perform maximally for a short period of time (less than 10 seconds - see Scheme AN1). The periods between the exercise bouts should be long enough for the muscles to recover to near resting conditions to enable a player to perform maximally in a subsequent exercise bout. For example, tests on professional Danish players showed that 25 seconds was not sufficient for them to recover fully after a seven-second sprint.

During speed training the players have to perform maximally in every phase of the drill.

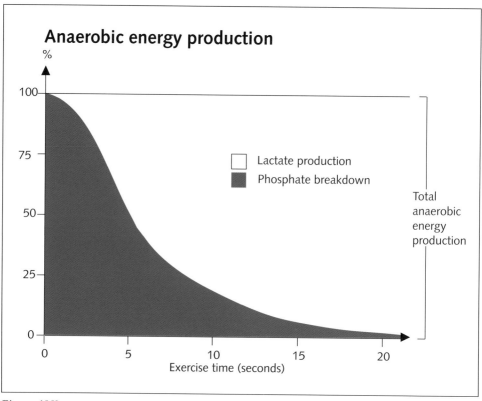

Figure AN2

The figure illustrates the relative contribution of anaerobic energy from breakdown of phosphates (shaded area) and from a process producing lactate (white area) during short-term intense exercise. The energy production from the use of phosphates accounts for a considerable part of the anaerobic energy production during bouts of exercise lasting less than 10 seconds.

Speed training should be performed at an early stage in a training session when the players are not tired. However, it is important that the players have warmed up thoroughly. When a speed training exercise is performed for 5-10 seconds it also improves speed endurance, since considerable amounts of lactate are produced. The greatest effect of speed training is, however, on the high energy phosphate system. Figure AN2 illustrates the relationship between the duration of exercise and the anaerobic energy production with and without lactate production.

Organisation

Speed training should mainly take the form of game-like situations - so-called functional speed training, since part of the desired training effect is to improve the players' ability to anticipate and react in different situations in soccer. Sprinting a set distance on a given command is an example of formal speed training. While this improves the ability to produce energy by the

140

anaerobic systems, it has little effect on the ability to react in soccer-specific situations. This is due to the fact that the players respond to signals, e.g. a whistle, that do not resemble the stimuli for action which occur during a match. In addition, during this type of speed training the muscles involved in other rapid movements in soccer are not trained sufficiently.

Formal speed training has traditionally been the predominant form of speed training in soccer. Thus players often associate speed training with sprinting without a ball. For psychological reasons it might therefore be necessary to include this form of training once in a while, although the overall effect for soccer is not optimal. The benefits may be improved with certain adaptations; for example, the start signal could be the bounce of a ball. One reason as to why formal speed training is popular, is that it is easy to organise and its objectives can be well defined, whereas the planning of functional speed training requires more imagination and the coach needs to continually assess whether the objectives of the training are being achieved. When selecting the form of speed training however, it should be recognised that the overall benefits from functional speed training are far greater than those that can be achieved by formal speed training.

Speed training drills

A number of drills suitable for functional speed training are described below.

Speed in a game is not only dependent on the ability of the muscles to produce energy rapidly but also related to the ability of a player to quickly perceive, evaluate, and decide.

Drill 1 – Catch (Fig. AN3)

Area: 10 x 60 metres.

Number of players: 10 (6-15).

Organisation: A server (S) is placed in the middle of two sets of cones positioned 40 metres apart. The players are lining up in a queue. One player at a time is sprinting.

Description: S passes to the player who returns the ball to S, who kicks it towards one of the sets of cones. The player sprints and tries to get the ball before it passes the cones (20 metres).

Rules: None

Scoring: The number of balls reached before the cones may be counted.

Variations: a. The distance of the sprints can be shortened, e.g. 10 metre, or increased, e.g. 30 metre.

b. S and the player pass to each other until S decides to kick the ball to one of the sets of cones.

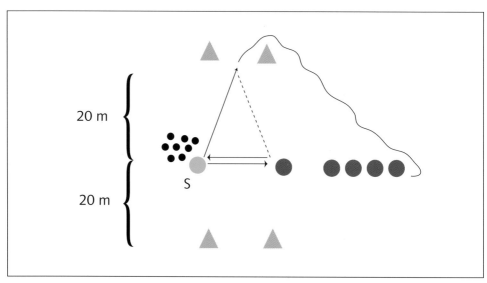

Catch (Fig. AN3)

c. The players are divided into pairs one attacker – and one defender. The attacker is positioned as in the original drill with the defender behind him. The attacker receives the ball from S and returns it, thereafter S plays it toward one of the sets of cones. The defender shall try to avoid the attacker dribbling through the goals. The players are taking turns in being attackers and defenders.

Hints for the coach: The players should not start out at maximal running speed. They may begin with a speed of 70% of maximal speed, followed by 80 and 90%. Then, the players should perform maximally in each sprint. S should try to kick with a force that gives the player a reasonable chance to reach the ball before the cones. The player must sprint all the way to the goal even though he cannot reach the ball. After a sprint the player should walk back and relax until he has to sprint again. The signal for the start of the sprint is the action of S, i.e. S's preparation for the kick, which is realistic for soccer. It is important that both S and the players are concentrated, which can be obtained if both are standing still before the sprint and if they have eye contact. It also helps if the other players stand several metres behind the player in action.

Variation a. varies the length of the sprints. One should keep in mind that most sprints in soccer last less than 3 seconds.

In variation b. the player needs to concentrate for a longer time, which is more demanding.

Variation c. will increase the level of competitiveness of the drill, and may increase the motivation of the players. The defender should not take chances, he should wait until he knows the direction of the attacker.

Drill 2 (Fig. AN 4)

Area: Half a soccer field with one full-size goal.

Number of players: 16 (4 - 22) + 1 goalkeeper.

Organisation: The players work in pairs. The drill may start from different positions on the field.

Description: Two players stand in front of a server. The server kicks the ball towards the goal. The players start to sprint immediately after the ball has been served. The player who reaches the ball first tries to score, i.e. becomes the attacker, while the other player becomes the defender.

Scoring: Ordinary scoring.

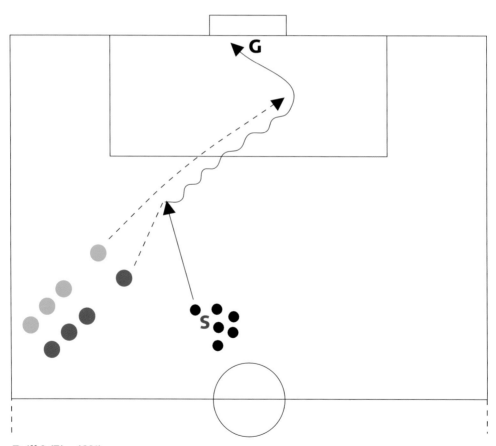

Drill 2 (Fig. AN4)

Variations:	a. Both players start with their backs to the goal, i.e. they are facing the server.
	b. One player starts in front of the other player (for example three metres apart) with the ball. The player with the ball is the attacker and must dribble with high speed towards the goal, the other player is a defender who must chase at maximal speed to try to prevent the attacker from scoring.
	c. The same as variation b., but the player must first dribble the ball around a cone.
	d. One player starts with the ball in front of the other player. The player makes a short wall pass to the server (who is nearer to the goal) and then attacks the goal. The defending player chases as in b.
Hints for the coach:	It is important that the players try hard to get to the ball first. The player who gains possession of the ball should be encouraged to make a direct run towards the goal and shoot. By varying the position of the serve, the players will need to concentrate throughout the exercise.

Drill 3 (Fig. AN5)

Area: A large circular area with a smaller inner circle, e.g. the centre-circle of a field.

Number of players: 10 (6 - 15).

Organisation: All players start with a ball inside the inner circle.

Description: The players dribble their ball inside the inner circle and attempt to kick the other balls out of this area. When a ball is kicked out of the inner circle, the player that had this ball must sprint to try to reach it before it rolls out of the outer circle. The player then walks back to the inner circle dribbling the ball.

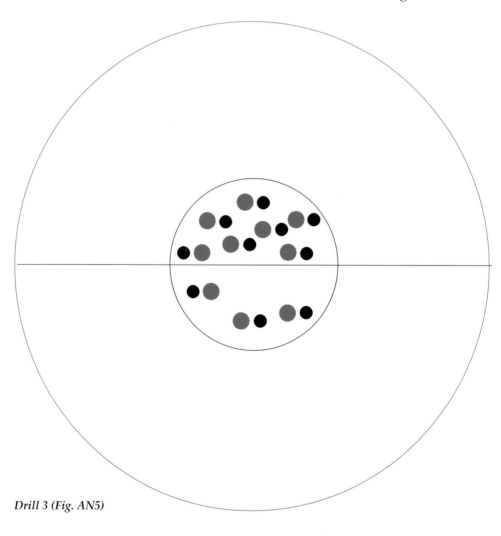

Drill 3 (Fig. AN5)

146

Rules:	None.
Scoring:	If the ball passes the outer circle the player that had the ball gets one negative point and the player that kicked it out gets one point. The player that has the most points after a certain time has won the game.
Variations:	a. The players are divided into two teams and should only try to kick out the opponents' balls. A point is scored for every ball kicked out of the outer circle. The player who has lost possession of the ball must sprint after it to try to stop it rolling out of the outer circle. The game is won by the team with the most points after a set game time.
	b. The players are divided into two teams. Each player on one team (attacking) starts with a ball inside the inner circle. The players of the other team (defending) have to be in the area between the perimeter of the inner circle and the perimeter of the outer circle. On a command from the coach the attacking players have a limited time, e.g. 10 seconds, to dribble the ball to the edge of the outer circle. The players of the defending team should try to prevent this. The teams alternate between attacking and defending. A point is scored for every player on the attacking team who reaches the edge of the outer circle in possession of a ball within the allocated time. The points are added up after a certain number of rounds and the game is won by the team with the most points.
Hints for the coach:	When a ball is kicked out of the inner circle, the player should be encouraged to immediately sprint after it to try to stop it rolling out of the outer circle. It is important that the players walk on their way back to the inner circle after a sprint so that they rest sufficiently.
	Using the variations a. and b. should help to make the game more competitive and thus increase the motivation of the players. Variation b. focus on high speed dribling.

Game 1 (Fig. AN6)

Area:
A soccer field with a middle-zone and two full-size goals.

Number of players:
3v3+6v6 (3v3+3v3 - 4v4+8v8) + 2 goalkeepers.

Organisation:
Three players from each team are „middle"-players who must not leave the middle zone. The remaining six players are „sprint"-players. After a set time the three „middle"-players change with three of the „sprint"-players from the same team.

Description:
The game consists of two sub-games.

Sub-game 1
The „middle"-players play 3v3 with one ball in the middle-zone (the „sprint"-players do not participate), where they defend and attack a row of cones. When a team knocks over one of its opponents´ cones then one of their own cones is transferred to the opponents´ row of the cones (see Scoring Cones, page 100).

Sub-game 2
A „middle"-player from sub-game 1 can at any time pass the ball out of the middle-zone towards one of the goals for one of the „sprint"-players (from the same team) to chase and try to score a goal. The „sprint"-player may only score if the ball is reached inside the shaded area (see Fig. AN 6). A player from the other team can also attempt to gain possession of the ball as soon as it leaves the middle-zone and, if successful, this player can score without any restrictions. Only one player from each team is allowed to compete for the balls passed from the middle-zone.

As soon as a ball is passed out of the middle-zone in sub-game 1, a „middle"-player from the opposing team runs to fetch a new ball which is positioned behind each team's row of cones (by the „sprint"-players), and the game is continued.

Rules: The goalkeepers must stay inside the penalty area.

Scoring: One point is given for knocking down a cone in sub-game 1 whereas three points are given for scoring a goal in sub-game 2. The game is won by the team with the most points after a set game time.

Variations:
a. Two players from each team may sprint after the ball.

b. Sub-game 1 is played with two balls at the same time.

148

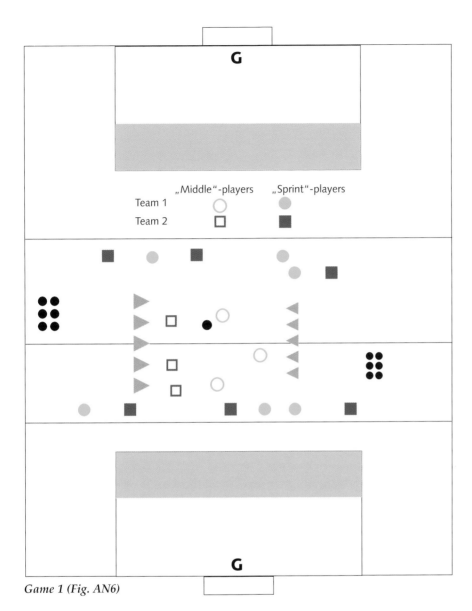

G

	„Middle"-players	„Sprint"-players
Team 1	○	●
Team 2	□	■

G

Game 1 (Fig. AN6)

Hints for the coach:

The task of the „middle"-players is to either knock down the opponents´ cones or to make an accurate pass so that one of their „sprint"-players can receive the ball inside the shaded area. The „sprint"-players must chase the ball or an opponent with maximum speed, but should walk back towards the middle zone after each sprint in order to recover.

The inclusion of variation a. will increase the number of sprints. However, the quality of each sprint may decrease if the subsequent rest periods are too short. Variation b. should increase the number of sprints as it will give the players in sub-game 1 more time and space to make a pass out of the middle-zone. It may be necessary to increase the number of players in sub-game 1 if this variation is used.

Speed endurance training

Aims

- To increase the ability to rapidly produce power and energy via anaerobic energy-producing systems.

- To increase the capacity to continuously produce power and energy through the anaerobic energy-producing systems.

- To increase the ability to recover after a period of high-intensity exercise.

Application to soccer

Findings of high blood lactate concentrations in top-class players during match-play indicate that the lactate producing energy system is highly stimulated during periods of a game (see page 22). Furthermore, analysis of matches has shown that the higher the level of soccer, the more high-speed running is performed (see Fig. AE9; page 106). The capacity to produce lactate and to repeatedly perform high-intensity exercise should therefore be specifically trained. This can be achieved through speed endurance training.

In order to examine the effect of speed endurance training on performance, a study was performed with players from a top-class Danish squad. Half of the players on the squad performed six weeks of functional speed endurance training, twice a week for 30 minutes per session, in addition to the normal training. The other half of the squad did not change their training. All players were tested before and after the six-week period using a soccer-specific field test. The testing showed that the players who performed speed endurance training had improved their test results after the training period, whereas the performance of the other players was unchanged (see Fig. AN7).

The lactate producing system should be trained in game-related actions.

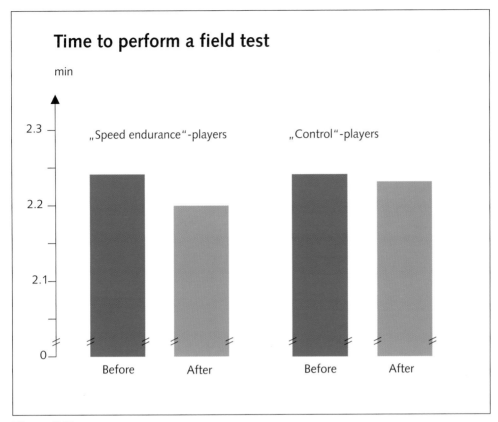

Figure AN7
The figure shows field test performance of two groups of top-class players tested twice during the season. In the period between the two tests, one group of players performed the ordinary training („Control"-players – on the right), whereas the other group performed their ordinary training combined with additional speed endurance training („Speed endurance"-players – on the left). The „Control"-players did not improve performance, whereas the „Speed endurance"-players had a better test result after the period.

Both the match analyses and the training study demonstrate that speed endurance training can be beneficial for soccer players. However, it is recommended that this type of training is only used with top-class players, as the training is very demanding both physically and mentally. When there is a limited amount of time available for training, time can be better utilised for other forms of training. To summarise:

● Speed endurance training can be effectively used for top-class players.

● Speed endurance training should have a low priority and may be completely omitted for non-elite players.

● Speed endurance training should not be used with players under 16 years of age.

Man-to-man contact requires a high rate of energy production from the anaerobic systems.

152

I. Maintenance training				
	Exercise (s)	Rest	Intensity	No. of repetitions
I a	10-90	As exercise duration	High-very high (45-100%)	2-10
I b	10-90	Aerobic low-intensity game for a maximal duration of 3 times exercise duration	High-very high (45-100%)	2-10

II. Production training				
	Exercise (s)	Rest	Intensity	No. of repetitions
II a	10-40	> 5 times exercise duration	Very high (70-100%)	2-10
II b	10-40	Aerobic low-intensity game for a minimum duration of 5 times exercise duration	Very high (70-100%)	2-10

Scheme AN2. Principles of speed endurance training

Principle

Speed endurance training can be divided into production training and maintenance training (sometimes called tolerance training). The purpose of production training is to improve the ability to perform maximally for a relatively short period of time, whereas the aim of maintenance training is to increase the ability to sustain exercise at a high intensity.

The exercise intensity during speed endurance training should be almost maximal, which means that the training must be performed according to an interval principle (see scheme AN2). During training games with exercise periods of 10-20 seconds it may be difficult to achieve the desired training effect, so exercise periods of more than 20 seconds are recommended if the traning is performed as game. In the production training the duration of the exercise bouts should be relatively short (10-40 seconds), and the rest periods in between the exercise bouts should be comparatively long (1-4 minutes) in order to maintain a very high intensity throughout the production training. In the maintenance training the exercise periods should be 10-90 seconds and the duration of the rest periods should approximately equal the exercise periods, so that the players progressively become fatigued. Scheme AN2 illustrates the principles of the two categories of anaerobic training.

If the exercise periods during speed endurance training last for one minute or more, heart rate measurements may be used to indicate whether or not the exercise intensity is high enough. Towards the end of such exercise periods heart rates should be close to maximum. Figure AN8 shows heart rate and blood lactate values for a player during and after the exercise periods in a speed endurance maintenance training session. The training was performed on a third of a field and consisted of a two-a-side game with man-to-man marking. One minute of exercise was interspersed by one minute of rest.

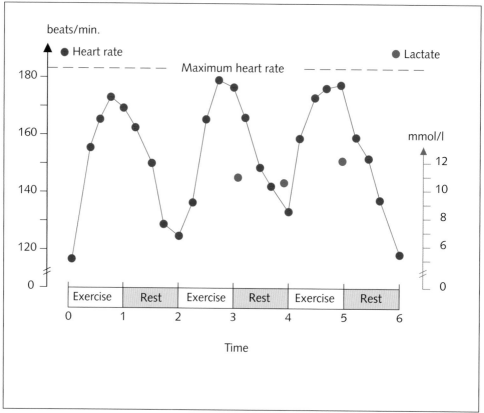

Figure AN8
The figure shows heart rate (●) and blood lactate concentration (●) of a player during a two-a-side training game with man-to-man on a third of the field. The player's heart rate approached maximum level towards the end of the one-minute work periods and decreased to about 120 beats/min during the rest periods. Blood lactate concentrations after the second and third exercise periods were 11 and 12 mmol/l, respectively, indicating a marked production of lactate. Thus, the drill served its purpose as a speed endurance maintenance training game.

Players during a speed endurance two-a-side training game (see also Fig. AN8)

Organisation

In reality, during speed endurance training games the players do not exercise at a maximum level of intensity throughout an exercise period. There are many factors that will affect the exercise intensity of a game, such as the tactical requirements. Figure CF10 (see page 26) shows examples of how the exercise intensity can vary for a player during speed endurance games.

To ensure that the exercise intensity is high throughout an exercise period, it is often necessary to motivate the players verbally, especially towards the end of the period. It is also important that there are enough balls available during the drills to minimise interruptions, which will interfere with the desired high tempo. In speed endurance training the rest periods between the bouts of high-intensity exercise should include recovery activities, e.g. players can jog to fetch the balls.

Speed endurance maintenance training should be conducted at the end of a training session, as the players will be physically affected for some time after this training. It is, however, important that the players perform some type of light exercise after the training to allow for rapid recovery.

Speed endurance training drills

A number of training drills which can be used for speed endurance training are described below. Some exercises without a ball are also given.

Speed endurance maintenance training drills

Game 1 – Attacking (Fig. AN9)

Area:	A quarter of a soccer field with one full-size goal.
Number of players:	2+2v2+2 (1+1v1+1) + 1 goalkeeper.
Organisation:	Each team consists of 2 x 2 players who take turns to play.
Description:	Ordinary soccer play with both teams attacking the same goal. The game is started by the server (S) passing a ball into the playing area. If a team loses possession of the ball by the goalkeeper catching it or if it is kicked out of the playing area, the next ball is served to the opposing team. After scoring a goal the same team gets the next ball from the server.
Rules:	None.
Scoring:	Ordinary scoring.
Type of exercise:	Fixed time intervals, e.g. an exercise period of 1-2 minutes with rest periods of the same duration.
Variations:	a. Use man-to-man marking.
	b. When a team gains possession of the ball, the ball must be taken into the green zone before attacking the goal (see Fig. AN9b).
	c. Only the players who are inside the green zone when the ball is played out of the green zone are allowed to participate in the following attack.
Hints for the coach:	It is important to continuously motivate the players to exercise at a high intensity. In variation a. the demands of the drill are further increased and a reduction in the duration of the exercise period may be necessary in order to maintain the desired exercise intensity. If one player cannot cope with the marking of an opponent, the intensity of the other two players can be affected, hence, it is important to have players of equal ability marking each other. Variation b. should decrease the number of shots and ensure that all players are exercising at a high intensity. In

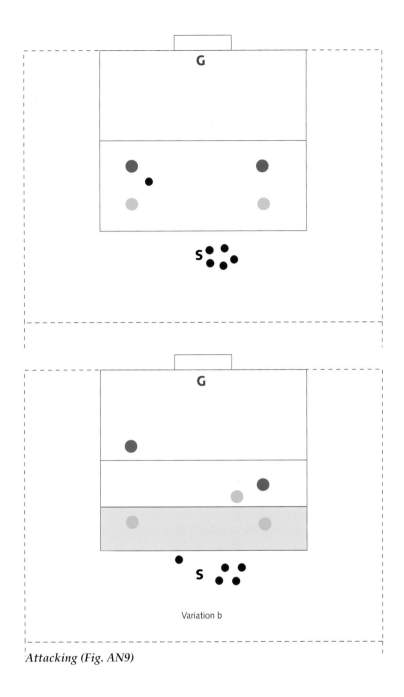

G

S

G

Variation b

Attacking (Fig. AN9)

variation c. the players must be aware that running back very fast prevents the opponents from interfering during the attack. This rule should ensure a higher overall exercise intensity, even though some players may be standing still for short periods. In variation c. reducing the size of the green area may further increase the physical demands.

Game 2 – Back and Forth (Fig. AN10)

Area:	A third of a soccer field with five small goals.
Number of players:	3+3v3+3 (2+2v2+2 - 4+4v4+4).
Organisation:	Each team has 2 x 3 players who take turns playing. Each team attacks and defends two of their own goals and a common goal in the middle of the field.
Description:	Ordinary soccer play. The team that gets the ball after a goal is scored continues the game, but the next scoring must be done in another goal. The players who are not playing support their own team by "wall-passes".
Rules:	None.
Scoring:	Scoring can be done both ways through a goal.
Type of exercise:	Fixed time intervals, e.g. exercise periods of one minute interspersed by one-minute rest periods.
Variations:	a. Man-to-man marking.
	b. A goal is scored by playing the ball through a goal to a team-mate on the other side of the goal.
Hints for the coach:	The players of the team that has possession of the ball should try to create space for themselves, while the opposing team should be encouraged to work hard to regain possession of the ball as quickly as possible. If the defending team adopts the tactic of having one player in each of the goals it may be necessary to increase the width of the goal or increase the number of goals. A larger distance between the goals should result in a higher overall exercise intensity. Variation a. should also increase the physical demands. However, the exercise intensity might be lower for some players if there is a large difference in the physical capacity of the two players who are marking each other. This problem can be partly solved by including variation b.

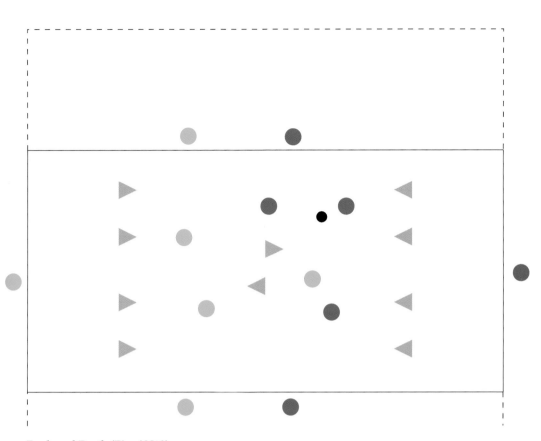

Back and Forth (Fig. AN10)

Game 3 – Combination (Fig. AN11)

Area:	A soccer field, divided into four zones - two middlezones (②+④) and two outer zones (①+③).
Number of players:	2x4v4 (2x3v3 - 2x5v5).
Organisation:	Four players from each team are in each of the two middle-zones. The game consists of two sub-games and begins with sub-game 1. At a given signal from the coach the players alternate between the two sub-games as indicated by the arrows and signs on Fig. AN11.
Description:	The game consists of two sub-games.

Sub-game 1
Goal Galore (see pge 120). Eight players play against eight with one ball in the two middle zones (4v4 in each zone). The players must try to keep possession of the ball within their team.

Sub-game 2
Goal Galore (see page 120).Four players play against four in the outer zones (①+③) The players must try to play the ball through the small goals (cones) to a team-mate.

Rules:	The players must stay inside their appointed zone during each of the sub-games. During sub-game 2 the players are not allowed to run through the goals.
Scoring:	In sub-game 1 a point is scored for making a set number of consecutive passes, e.g. 10, without the other team touching the ball. In sub-game 2, a point is scored for passing the ball through one of the goals to a team-mate.
Type of exercise:	Fixed time intervals, e.g. in sub-game 2 the exercise period can be 90 seconds, while in sub-game 1 it can be three minutes.
Variations:	a. Use man-to-man marking in sub-game 2.
	b. Scoring during sub-game 2 is only allowed if the receiving player makes a first time pass to a team-mate and the pass does not go through the goal.

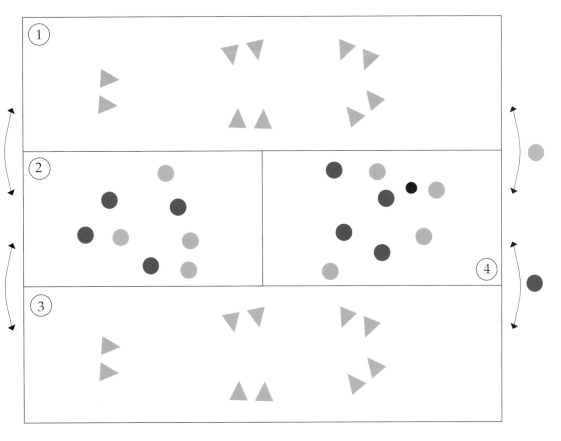

Combination (Fig. AN11)

Hints for the coach: The actual speed endurance maintenance training occurs in sub-game 2 in which the players should be encouraged to exercise at a very high intensity. Sub-game 1 allows the players to recover from sub-game 2. Therefore, the tempo in sub-game 1 should be relatively low, but the players should be encouraged to keep moving. The exercise demands in sub-game 2 can be controlled by changing both the number and width of the goals. Variation a. should increase the overall exercise intensity in sub-game 2. Variation b. can also increase the exercise intensity and is effective if one team has scored several more goals than the other team.

Exercise without a ball

Exercise 1 – Slalom (Fig. AN12)

Area:	Half a soccer field.
Number of players:	Unlimited. A team consists of three or four players.
Organisation:	Cones are positioned as shown in Fig. AN12 and each team starts between two cones.
Description:	Each player runs with a dispatch, e.g. a vest. At a given signal the first player follows the route illustrated in Fig AN12 back to the start where the dispatch is passed to a team-mate, who repeats the run. This continues until each player has performed a set number of runs, e.g. three runs per player.
Scoring:	The game is won by the team that finishes the set number of runs first.
Type of exercise:	Intermittent, e.g. exercise periods of approximately one minute with two-minute rest periods. Total duration, e.g. 23 minutes (two rounds consisting of three runs with approximately five minutes between each round).
Variation:	Players start at both ends of the row of cones and pass the dispatch accordingly.
Hints for the coach:	The players should run almost maximally during each shuttle. To keep the players motivated it is important that the teams are as equal as possible in terms of fast and slow players. The variation will shorten both the exercise time and the duration of the rest periods.

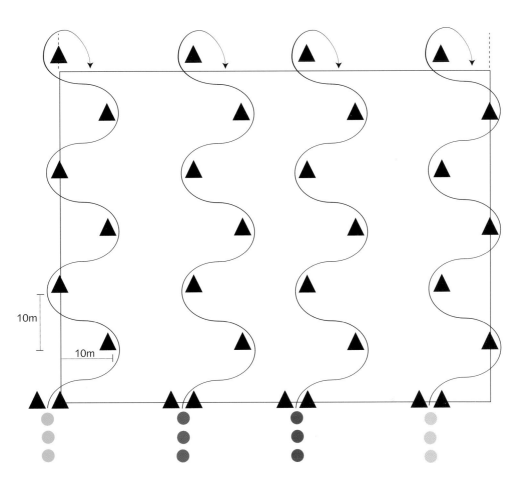

10m

10m

Slalom (Fig. AN12)

Speed endurance production training drills

Drill 1 – Hunting (Fig. AN13)

Area: A small circular area (radius approximately three metres) inside a large circular area (radius approximately 20 metres).

Number of players: 5 (4-8).

Organisation: A server (S), a „speed endurance" player (SE), and a minimum of two balls. The players take turns exercising.

Description: The server plays a ball towards the perimeter of the outer circle (1). SE must try to stop the ball rolling out of the outer circle. SE then dribbles the ball back into the inner circle at maximal speed. The server plays another ball as soon as SE is back inside the inner circle (2).

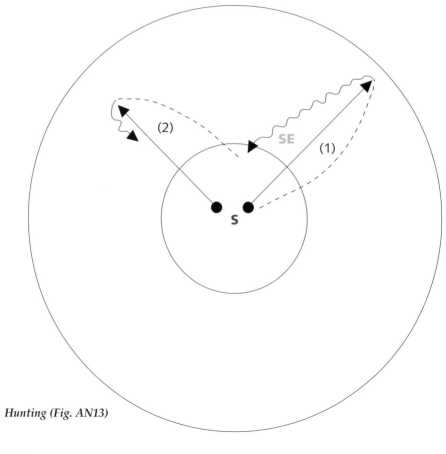

Hunting (Fig. AN13)

Rules: None.

Scoring: The number of balls that SE stops from rolling out of
                       the outer circle.

Type of exercise: Fixed time intervals, e.g. exercise periods of 20-30
                       seconds and rest periods of 2-3 minutes.

Variations: a. Only one ball is used. SE chases the ball and
                          passes it directly back to the server, who then
                          serves it with a first-time pass.

                       b. Two players compete for the ball. The player that
                          gets the ball should try to pass the ball back to the
                          server whereby one point is received. The other
                          player must try to prevent the pass. The server
                          either serves with a first-time pass as in variation
                          a. or serves a new ball.

Hints for the coach: It is important that the exercise is performed at close
                       to maximum intensity. The server can control the
                       overall demands of the drill and should give SE a
                       realistic chance of reaching the ball before it rolls out
                       of the outer circle. In variation a. and b. the ball
                       should be played back to the server as quickly as
                       possible, otherwise the overall exercise intensity
                       may be too low. An effective method of ensuring that
                       the ball is played back quickly is to restrict the
                       number of ball touches to a maximum of three. Extra
                       balls should be kept ready in case the back pass is
                       missed.

Drill 2 – Shooting (Fig. AN14)

Area:	A third of a soccer field with one full-size goal.
Number of players:	6 (5-8) + 1 goalkeeper.
Organisation:	A server (S), a „speed endurance" player (SE), a cone, and several balls. The players take turns exercising.
Description:	The server passes a ball to SE who shoots at the goal and then runs around the cone before the next shot.
Rules:	None.
Scoring:	The number of goals scored within a set time.
Type of exercise:	Fixed time intervals, e.g. exercise periods of 20 seconds and rest periods of 2.5 minutes (i.e. 5 x 20 + 5 x 10 seconds).
Variations:	a. SE receives the ball in the air and either shoots directly or after being in control of the ball.
	b. SE may dribble around the goalkeeper.
	c. SE takes free-kicks (i.e. the server positions the ball every time).
Hints for the coach:	The players should be encouraged to sprint around the cone immediately after their attempt at the goal. In variation b. it may be necessary to restrict the number of ball touches, e.g. a maximum of six, in order to prevent the exercise intensity from becoming too low.

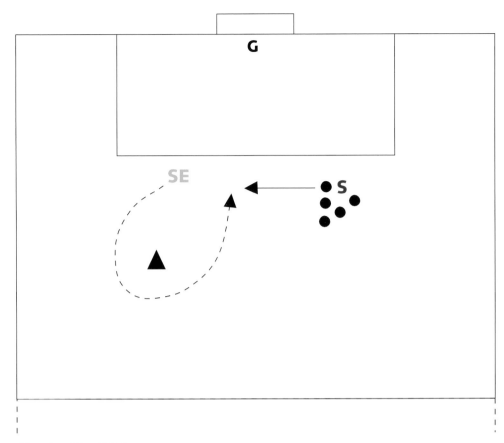

Shooting (Fig. AN14)

Game 4 – Chaos (Fig. AN15)

Area:	Half a soccer field with two full-size goals.
Number of players:	6v6 (5v5 - 9v9) + 2 goalkeepers.
Organisation:	Several balls are scattered around the field. The game consists of two sub-games and starts with sub-game 1. At a given signal the players change between the two sub-games. After sub-game 2 the balls must be scattered around the playing area again.
Description:	The game consists of two sub-games.
	Sub-game 1 Ordinary soccer with one ball and normal scoring.
	Sub-game 2 All the balls may be used. The players should within a given time try to score as many goals (in the opponents´ goal) as possible, using the balls that are scattered around the edge of the playing area (if a goal is scored the ball must stay inside the goal until the end of that period). Each team should also try to prevent the opposing team from scoring.
Rules:	None.
Scoring:	A goal is worth five points in sub-game 1 and one point in sub-game 2.
Type of exercise:	Intermittent. Sub-game 1 can be performed for a period of around five minutes while the duration of sub-game 2 may last up to 40 seconds.
Variations:	a. Both teams are divided into defenders and attackers in sub-game 2. The defenders should try to prevent the opposing attackers from scoring and vice-versa.
	b. During sub-game 2 the players work in pairs and play against a pair of opponents, with one ball at a time.
	c. During sub-game 2 a player from the attacking team can only score if inside the goal area.

168

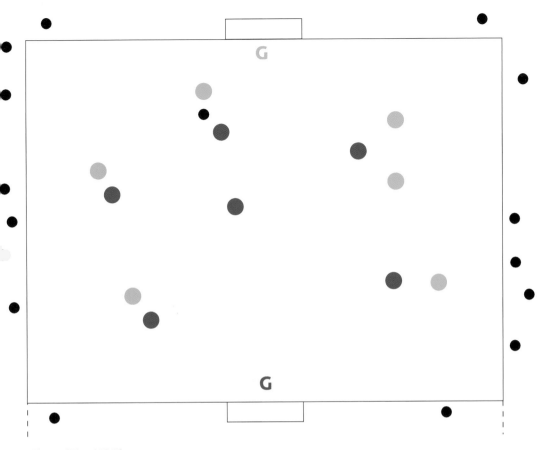

Chaos (Fig. AN15)

Hints for the coach: During sub-game 2 the exercise intensity must be almost maximal (speed endurance production training). The coach should emphasise that hard work can be rewarded by more goals. Initially sub-game 2 might appear rather disorganised, but, generally, the players quickly understand the idea of the game. During sub-game 1 the exercise intensity should be relatively low, which may be obtained by reducing the size of the playing area or by increasing the number of players. Variations a. and b. should increase the overall demand. Variation c. may be used if the intensity during sub-game 2 is too low because the players are trying to score with long shots.

Exercise without a ball

Exercise 2 – Relay Race (Fig. AN16)

Area:	A soccer field or a similar area.
Number of players:	15 (three teams of five players).
Organisation:	A cone is positioned behind each of the goals, in the corners and at the points where the centre-line and the side-lines meet. One player from each team stands at the cones at the sidelines and at the goallines. The extra player in each team is positioned at the starting cone.
Description:	At a signal, one of the players at the starting cone runs in a clock-wise direction along the sidelines of the field. This player carries a dispatch, e.g. a vest, which is passed to the team-mate at the next cone.
Type of exercise:	Intermittent, e.g. exercise periods for each player of approximately 15 seconds with 60-second rest periods. Total duration, e.g. 3 x 5 minutes (three entire rounds per player).
Scoring:	The team that first completes the set number of rounds has won.
Hints for the coach:	The players should perform maximally in each run. To keep the players motivated it is important that the teams are as equal as possible in terms of fast and slow players.

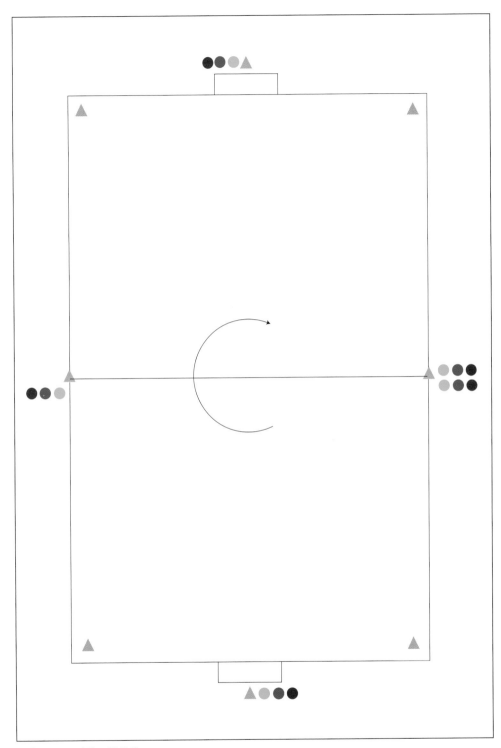

Relay Race (Fig. AN16)

Summary

Anaerobic training consists of speed training and speed endurance training, of which the latter can be divided into production training and maintenance training.

In soccer, speed is not merely dependent on physical capacity, but also involves rapid decision making which must then be translated into quick movements. Therefore, the aim of speed training is also to improve a player's ability to perceive, evaluate, and act quickly in match situations where speed is essential. In order to obtain this effect speed training should mainly be performed with a ball.

Speed endurance training increases the muscle's ability to rapidly produce force and improves the capacity of muscles to maintain a high power output. This type of training can enable a player to exercise at a high intensity more frequently and for longer periods of time. This ability is especially important for top-class players.

Planning the Season

Soccer players need a high level of fitness to cope with the physical demands of a game and to allow for their technical skills to be utilised throughout a match. Therefore, fitness training is an important part of the overall training programme. However, the amount of emphasis placed on fitness training depends on several factors, such as the players' competency in other areas of the game (see Fig. PL1, page 174), and the exercise intensity during training sessions which are not specifically designed to develop fitness. The type of training and the total loading of a player, in particular at a high level, should also be taken into account. Every player, independent of level of soccer, has a zone of optimal training stimuli as illustrated in Fig. PL2 (see page 175). This means that the player will have the greatest effect of training in this zone, if he trains less he will not improve enough and if he trains more it will only have a moderate effect („overloading"). If „overloading" occurs over weeks it can lead to a state of „overtraining", which is characterised by a marked decrease in performance for a prolonged period of time.

When planning fitness training the phases of the playing season should be taken into account. A year can be divided into a pre-season, a season, and a mid-season break. This chapter will focus on how to prioritise the various areas of fitness training throughout the year with a special emphasis on how to prepare for a tournament. It should be emphasised that due to specific demands of players in a team there may be major deviations in the priority of the aspects of fitness training. Furthermore, a coach should be prepared to change or adjust a planned training session at any time, e.g. it may sometimes be appropriate to avoid intensive fitness training in order to allow the players to rest mentally and physically. One of the sections will therefore deal with how to maintain the fitness level in periods with reduced training

Pre-season

The term „pre-season" covers the period between the last match of one season and the first match of the next. The pre-season can be divided into a maintenance period and a re-building period. The maintenance period is from the last match of the previous season to the resumption of team training, and the re-building period is from the resumption of team training until the first match of the next season. The duration of these periods varies from country to country. In some countries the maintenance period is about eight weeks and the re-building period five to eight weeks. In other countries the total pre-season period is four to six months with a maintenance period of two to three months.

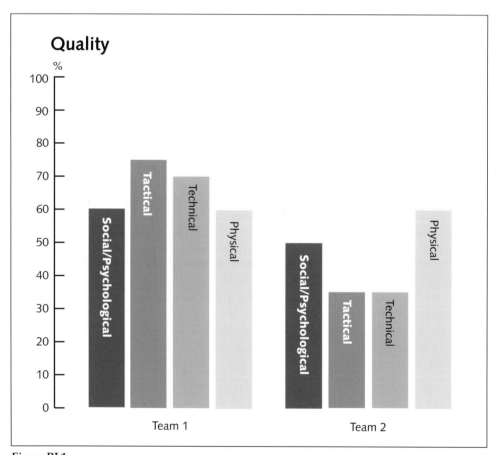

Figure PL1
The figure shows a hypothetical example of how two teams differ in quality within the four main areas of soccer, i.e. social/psychological, tactical, technical, and physical. The two teams are of the same fitness level but team 1 is superior in the other areas. Therefore, team 1 should spend more time on fitness training than team 2, which should focus on improving its tactical and technical abilities.

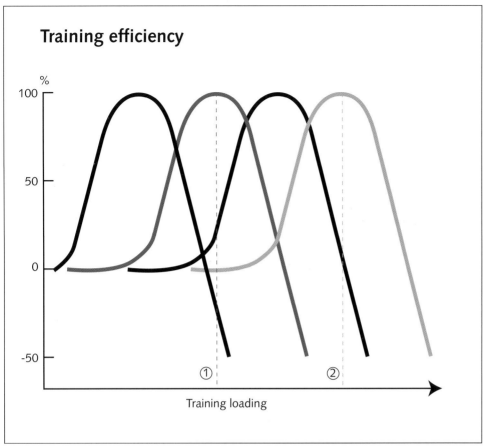

Figure PL2
The figure illustrates the training efficiency for players with a different training potential. As an example, player ① may get an optimal training stimulus if he trains twice a week, each session lasting 90 minutes, including aerobic high intensity training and anaerobic training. If player ② carries out the same amount and type of training he will not have any improvements. Player ② may need to train 5 times per week to reach a sufficient stimulus to increase performance. On the other hand, if player ① did that amount of training he would suffer from „overloading".

Traditionally, the maintenance period has been used for mental recovery with very little physical training, and the first month of the re-building period has focused mainly on fitness training with an emphasis on long distance running and muscle endurance training. The training at the beginning of the re-building period has often been very intensive, as coaches want to ensure that players reach „top form" for the start of the competitive season. This can partly explain why a high frequency of injuries occurs during this period. A more efficient way of planning the pre-season training is described below.

The maintenance period
(from the end of one season to approximately eight weeks
before the start of the next season)

By maintaining a certain amount of endurance training after the end of the season, the decrease in fitness, which always occurs after cessation of normal training and competition, will be minimised. This means that the players will have a good basic fitness level for the start of the re-building period. In order to help the players to relax mentally, parts of the training in the maintenance period can consist of other ball games, e.g. field hockey or basketball. The number of training sessions per week is dependent on many factors, but between one and four times per week, with additional individual training, may be suitable. During the last month before the re-building period the training frequency should be increased to at least two sessions per week.

Detailed planning
An example of the training frequency and exercise intensity for non-professional players during a week in the maintenance period is illustrated in Scheme PL1. The intensity of the training is represented by a number (scale: 1-5). A higher number indicates a higher intensity. Training with intensity 3 or 4 in the maintenance period should be regarded as training with the main aim of improving or maintaining the level of fitness.

Week Schedule – Maintenance period

Day/Time period	0-15	15-30	30-45	45-60	60-75	minutes
Monday	Warm-up	3	3	4	3	Recovery activities
Thursday	Warm-up	3	3	3	4	Recovery activities

Scheme PL1
Explanation of codes: *3 = Moderate intensity*   *4 = High intensity*

The re-building period
(approximately eight weeks before the start of the season)

During the re-building period fitness training should mainly consist of games and exercises with a ball. This ensures that the relevant muscles are being trained, and allows for technical and tactical aspects to be practised under physically taxing conditions. As the start of the season approaches, the number of training sessions should be gradually increased. In some countries the playing surface is changed (e.g. sand/gravel to grass) during the re-building period which can cause problems for the players as their muscles are stressed in a different way. In order to decrease the risk of injury the transition between playing surfaces should be gradual.

During the re-building period training matches are a good and appropriate form of fitness training, but they should not be played before the players are prepared physically for the demands of a full match.

Training camps
Clubs often organise a training camp or tour during the re-building period. This may be for a week or just a couple of days. Unfortunately, many coaches consider training camps to be a good opportunity to develop high levels of fitness, and therefore include up to three intensive training sessions per day. This is a mistake, which invariably results in many injuries. Many teams, including top-class teams, return from training camps with several injured players and a group of players who are both physically and mentally exhausted.

Training camps should be renamed „recovery" camps, and fitness training should not be the most important aspect of such a camp. Having the team assembled for an extended period of time can have many benefits. Since the players are together under less stressful circumstances than normally, it can enhance team spirit, and more time can be spent on developing technical skills and tactical strategies, both in theory and practice.

Detailed planning
An example of the training frequency and exercise intensity for a typical week for a non-professional team during the re-building period is illustrated in Scheme PL2 (the total duration of a training session is 90 minutes).

Week Schedule – Re-building period

Day/Time period	0-15	15-30	30-45	45-60	60-75	75-90	minutes
Monday	Warm-up	3	3	4	3	3	Recovery activities
Tuesday	Warm-up	3	5	3	4	3	Recovery activities
Thursday	Warm-up	3	5	2	4	3	Recovery activities
Saturday	Warm-up			Training match			

Scheme PL2
Explanation of codes:
2 = Low intensity, 3 = Moderate intensity,
4 = High intensity, 5 = Very high intensity

Players working in „station".

The intensity of the training is represented by a number (1-5). A higher number indicates a higher intensity. Only periods with an intensity of 4 or 5 should be considered as fitness training, i.e. training which is performed with the main purpose of improving the physical capacity of the players. During periods with an intensity of 2 or 3, priority is placed on other areas of the game, such as tactical strategy.

It may be advantageous for players to work in smaller groups during the re-building period. A training model which is easy to organise and which can also have a motivating effect on the players is „station"-training. Figure PL3 shows three examples of how „station"-training may be organised. There are 3 or 4 stations where either an aerobic moderate or high intensity game is played.

178

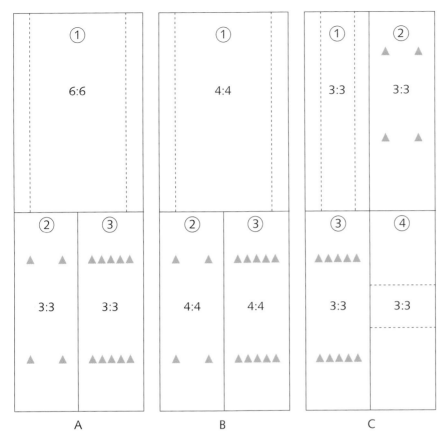

Figure PL3

The figure gives three examples of how „station training" can be organised. There are three stations in A and B, and four in C. Twenty-four players are divided into two teams.

In A there are 12 players (six from each team) at station ①, and six players (three from each team) at station ② and ③. After a given time-period the players change stations. The players from stations ② and ③ rotate to station ①, while the players from station ① advance to station ② and ③. After one more period, the players from stations ② and ③ return to station ①, while the players from station ① go to the station where they have not yet been. With this kind of organisation the players will have the same six opponents.

In B there are eight players (four from each team) at each station, and in C there are six players (three from each team) at each of the four stations. When changing stations in B and C, the two teams at a station move in opposite directions so that the opponents change (the players will meet again).

The players may alternate between performing an aerobic moderate and high intensity game. This can be achieved by performing aerobic moderate intensity games at stations ② and ③, and aerobic high intensity games at stations ① and ④. Examples of games:

Station 1: Pendulum (see page 122)
Station 2: Ordinary soccer play but with scoring both from in front of and from behind a goal.
Station 3: Scoring cones (see page 100)
Station 4: Deep (see page 114)

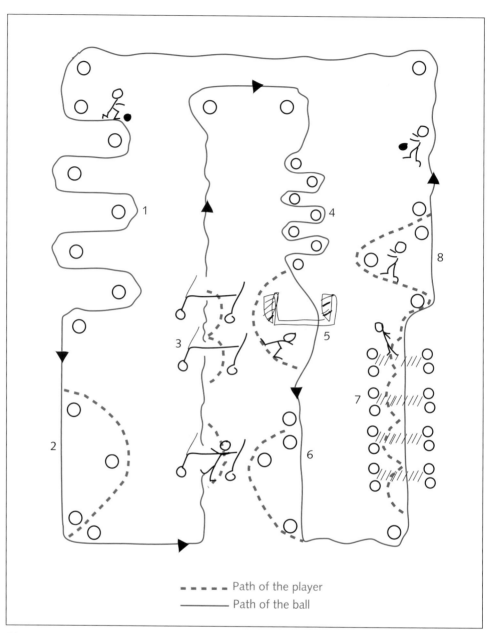

Figure PL4

The figure shows an example of an obstacle course that can be performed with a ball. The solid-line (——) shows the path of the ball and the dotted-line (----) illustrates the course of the player.

Explanation of codes:

1: slalom dribbling; 2: passing the ball forward and meeting it again after running around the cones; 3: passing the ball forward and then jumping over hurdles; 4: same as 1; 5: passing the ball over a big goal and retrieving it on the other side; 6: same as 2: 7: passing the ball forward and meeting it after jumping across the marked areas; 8: same as 2.

If bad weather prevents access to a good playing surface, the players can run with the ball around an obstacle course. This type of training easily motivates players, and at the same time they exercise using movements specific to soccer. An example of an obstacle course is shown in Fig. PL4.

Effect of pre-season training
A top-class Danish team followed a pre-season training schedule similar to the one described above. Six weeks before the start of the re-building period the players trained twice a week. The training frequency during the re-building period was gradually increased to five times per week. The fitness level of the players was evaluated with a number of tests before and after the re-building period. The results of these tests are shown in Fig. PL5 and are compared to results obtained during the season. Although the increase in maximum oxygen uptake was rather small during the re-building period, the level obtained was almost as high as that during the

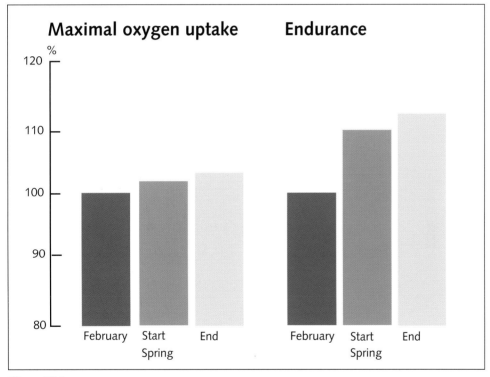

Figure PL5

The figure shows the maximum oxygen uptake and the endurance capacity of players on a Danish elite team on three occasions during the year: towards the end of February – just before the players started the re-building period; in the beginning of April – just after the start of the season; and in the middle of June – during the first half of the season. The values are expressed in relation to those obtained in February (100%). During the re-building period the maximum oxygen uptake and endurance capacity were only slightly lower than during the season. Thus, the short re-building period was sufficiently long for the players to reach a high fitness level.

season. More impressive was the large increase in endurance capacity during the re-building period. The ability of the players to exercise for prolonged periods of time was almost as good at the start of the season as it was during the season. This demonstrates that it is possible for the players to have a high level of fitness before the start of the season by means of this structuring of the pre-season period. When the season started the team had no injured players and went on to win the first three matches.

Tests results from players in the a Danish club, who were competing in the UEFA Cup, also demonstrate that it is possible to reach a high level of fitness in a relatively short period of time, provided that the initial fitness level is already fairly high. These players were tested three times during the year: in early January before an intensive preparation period for a European Cup quarter-final match, in early March, a few days before this match, and in October during the season. The results showed that the players´ physical capacity at the time before the match was just as high as during the season (see Fig. PL6).

These studies demonstrate that soccer players can reach peak physical performance at the beginning of the season, even with a short re-building period (5-8 weeks) in the club. However, this is assuming that there has not

During the pre-season it is important that the players have a lot of contakt with the ball.

182

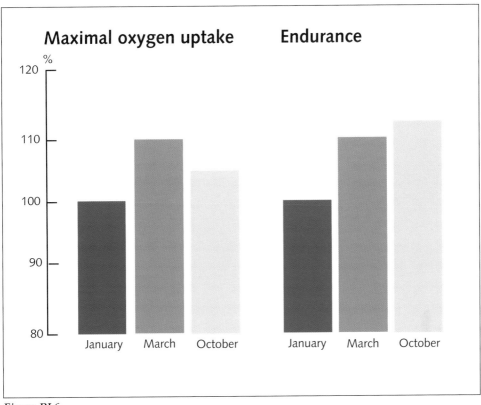

Figure PL6

The figure shows the maximum oxygen uptake and the endurance capacity of players in a Danish professional team on three occasions: in the beginning of January – just prior to the start of the re-building period; in the middle of March – just before a UEFA Cup match; and in October – during the second half of the season. The values are expressed in relation to those obtained in January (100%)

been a marked decrease in the physical capacity during the maintenance period.

Beginning the re-building period with a relatively high fitness level will allow for a slow development of the players´ physical capacity when club training starts again, and time can be spent on improving other performance characteristics in soccer, e.g. technical skills. By a gradual transition between individual training out of the club and the training at the club, the muscles are well prepared for high-intensity exercise. In this way muscle soreness, which is especially common after the first training sessions during the start of the re-building period, can be avoided. The risk of getting injured is reduced and the players are often well-motivated when training eventually becomes more intensive. In addition, there is a lower risk of both mental and physical „overtraining". In northern countries where pre-season training occurs in the winter, postponing the re-building period means that fewer training sessions will be performed under difficult weather conditions.

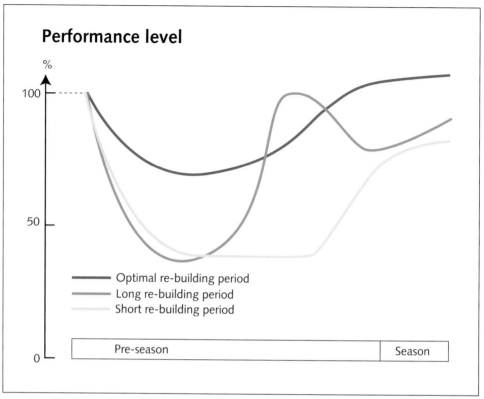

Figure PL7
The figure provides a theoretical illustration of the changes in a player's fitness level as a result of structuring the pre-season in the way recommended in the text (▬▬). Also included are the changes in fitness level with two other programmes in which no training was performed during the maintenance period, and the re-building period was either long (▬▬▬) or short (▬▬).

By maintaining a certain level of activity during the maintenance period, the decrease in fitness level after the season is reduced and the players can reach peak performance and even a higher performance level than last season with a relatively short re-building period. With a long and intense re-building period the players may peak before the season, whereas with a short re-building period the players may not have a sufficient fitness level at the start of the season, if they do not train during the maintenance period.

Figure PL7 shows changes in physical performance during the pre-season with three different forms of planning. A comparison is made between the changes in physical performance achieved by pre-season training according to the above suggested planning, and programmes with no training during the maintenance period and with either a shorter or longer re-building period.

In periods with many training sessions and games, the players can recover mentally by performing other activities.

From the early phase of the re-building period it is important to prioritise aerobic high intensity training and about six weeks before the season speed training, and for elite players, speed endurance training should also be included. The effect of these types of training on the players´ ability to repeatedly perform intense exercise can be evaluated by performing the Yo-Yo intermittent recovery test and a repeated sprint test (for further information see „Fitness testing in soccer“). These test were used to examine the effect of the training in the re-building period for two professional teams reaching the second and third position in the Danish Premier league three months later. Figures PL8 and PL9 show that the players had a marked improvement in the ability to perform intense intermittent exercise and also increased sprint performance, independent of position in the team. Apparently the aerobic high intensity training and anaerobic training had been effective in improving these performance parameters.

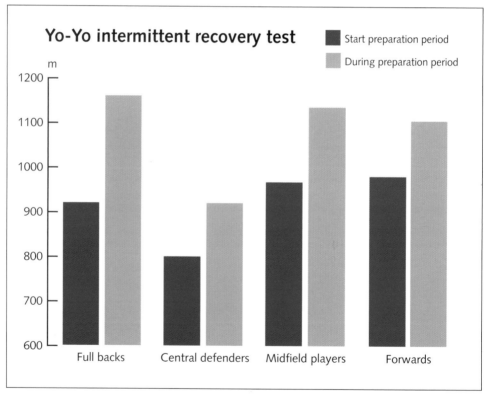

Figure PL8

The figure shows performance in the Yo-Yo intermittent recovery test of 36 Danish professional players in different positions determined at the start of the re-building period and six weeks later, two weeks before the start of the season. It is clear that all players groups had significant improvements and that the players reached a level close to what is observed for top-class teams in Europe.

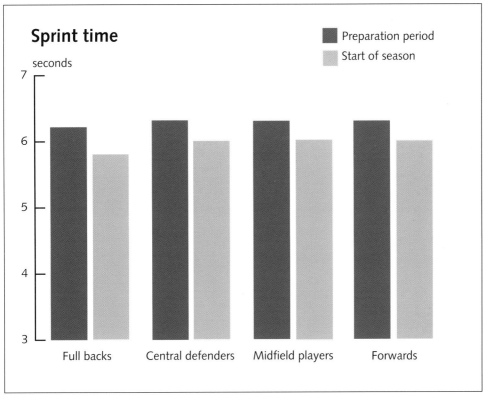

Figure PL9
The figure shows sprint performance of 36 Danish professional players in different positions determined at the start of the re-building period and eight weeks later at the start of the season. In each group a significant improvement was observed suggesting the speed training had been effective.

Summary – Pre-season

The pre-season period can be divided into a maintenance period and a re-building period. During the maintenance period mainly aerobic moderate intensity training should be performed to ensure a good physical foundation before the start of the re-building period (see Scheme PL3, page 188). During the re-building period the players should have frequent sessions of aerobic high intensity training, speed training, and for elite players, speed endurance training (see Scheme PL3, page 188). After the first two-three weeks of the re-building period the team should regularly play matches at a high competitive level. Training camps are recommended but should not be used primarily to increase the physical capacity of the players.

	Maintenance period		Pre-season Re-building period	
Aerobic				
Moderate-intensity training	3344*	4444	4455	4443
High-intensity training	2223	3234	4445	4555
Anaerobic				
****Speed endurance training**	1111	1111	2334	4555
Speed training	1111	1111	2344	4555

Scheme PL3

Explanation of codes:

1 = Very low priority (need not be trained)
2 = Low priority (may be trained).
3 = Moderate priority (should preferably be trained).

4 = High priority (should be trained).
5 = Very high priority (must be trained).

Scheme PL3 indicates how much priority should be given to the individual forms of training during the maintenance and re-building periods. The higher the number (1-5), the more important the training form.

Season

During the season the level of fitness achieved during the re-building period should be maintained and perhaps even improved.

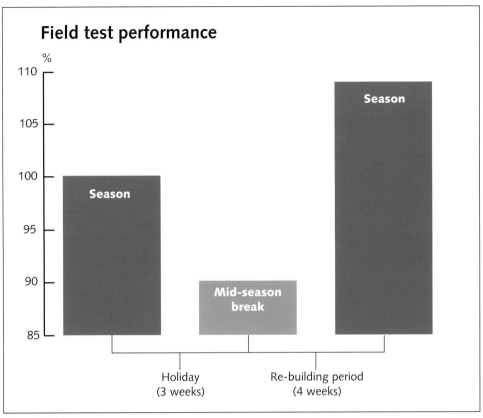

Figure PL10
The figure shows performance in a field test performed during the season, after three weeks of holiday, and after a four-week re-building period (start of the second half of the season). The values are expressed in relation to the level during the season (100%)

The players showed a better performance after the re-building period compared to during the season, suggesting that the players' ability to perform intense exercise was not high enough during the season. For further results from this study see Fig. PL 13 (see page 194).

Studies have shown that there is a relationship between the standard of play and the amount of high-speed running during a match, so players should have a high ability to repeatedly perform intense exercise. This capacity can be maintained and improved by aerobic high-intensity training and anaerobic training. Coaches do not always put sufficient emphasis on these types of training during the season. In a study with Danish top-class players, the effect of a seven-week mid-season break consisting of three weeks of holiday followed by a four-week re-building period was evaluated. After the re-building period, the players were better at performing high-intensity exercise compared to before the mid-season break (see Fig. PL10). Apparently the intensity of the training during the first half of the season had not been high enough. In another study with Danish top-class players, heart rate was measured during several matches and during the type of training

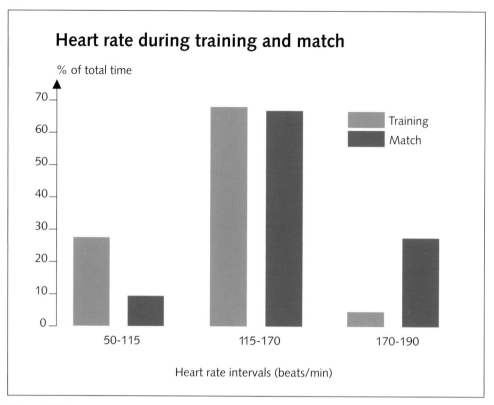

Heart rate during training and match

Figure PL11

The figure compares heart rate of Danish top-class players during fitness training and during a match. The values are expressed in percent of training time and match time, respectively. The time periods when heart rate was between 50-115 (to the left), 115-170 (in the middle), and 170-190 beats/min (to the right) are shown. It is clear that the players' heart rates were consistently higher during the matches compared to the training, indicating that the exercise intensity during the training was too low.

which the coach considered to be the most physically demanding. During the matches the heart rate was on average higher than 170 beats/min for about 25% of the game, while the corresponding period during training was 4% (see Fig. PL11). Thus, the exercise intensity during the fitness training was considerably lower than the intensity during the matches.

The endurance capacity of players may be maintained by regularly supplementing the match programme with prolonged training sessions (once or twice per week) that include aerobic moderate-intensity games. It is essential that the exercise intensity is fairly high and that there are only short interruptions during the sessions.

Week schedule – Season

Day/ Time period	0-15	15-30	30-45	45-60	60-75	75-90	minutes
Monday	Warm-up	3	3	3	Recovery activities		
Tuesday	Warm-up	3	5	3	4	3	Recovery activities
Thursday	Warm-up	5	2	4	4	3	Recovery activities
Saturday	Warm-up	2	3	2	Recovery activities		
Sunday	Warm-up				Match		

Scheme PL4
Explanation of codes:
2 = Low intensity.
3 = Moderate intensity.
4 = High intensity.
5 = Very high intensity.

Detailed planning
An example of the training frequency and intensity for a typical week during the season is illustrated in Scheme PL4. The intensity of the training is represented by a number (1-5). A higher number indicates a higher intensity.

The schedule presented is representative of a training pattern for a non-professional team with four training sessions per week. A team that trains twice a week can follow the training intensities for Tuesday and Thursday. Naturally, the absolute training intensity will be lower than that expected of an elite team, but the general outline can still be followed.

For a top-class club with part-time or full-time professionals, it is reasonable to include Wednesday as an extra training day. Training twice per day may be performed on certain days, e.g. Tuesday and/or Thursday. For the top-class players it is important to get adequate rest, and to eat and drink properly between training sessions (see the book "Nutrition in Soccer"). Some of the training sessions should be less demanding, e.g. practise of free-kicks and corners.

	Season						
	First half				Second half		
Aerobic							
Moderate-intensity training	4343*	4343	433	343	4343	4343	4343
High-intensity training	5555	5555	555	555	5555	5555	5444
Anaerobic							
**Speed endurance trining	3453	4534	543	453	4534	5345	3453
Speed training	5555	5555	555	555	5555	5555	5544

Scheme PL5

Explanation of codes:
1 = Very low priority (need not be trained).
2 = Low priority (may be trained).
3 = Moderate priority (should preferably be trained).
4 = High priority (should be trained).
5 = Very high priority (must be trained).
* see the book "Fitness traning..."
** see the book "Fitness traning..."

Summary – season
Aerobic high intensity training should be given a high priority during a season. Speed training, and for top-class players, speed endurance training, should also be performed regularly. Endurance capacity may be maintained by frequently including prolonged training sessions with only short rest periods. Scheme PL5 indicates how much priority should be given to each form of training during the season. The higher the number (1-5), the more important the type of training.

Mid-season break

In some countries the season is divided into two halves separated by a mid-season break, which can be from four to 18 weeks. Like the pre-season, the mid-season break can be divided into a maintenance period and a re-building period.

A study was conducted with a top-class Danish club in an attempt to clarify how much and what type of training should be performed during these periods. The players were monitored before, during, and after a seven-week mid-season break. The players did not train during the first three weeks, and during the following four weeks they trained with a main focus on improving physical capacity (see Fig. PL12).

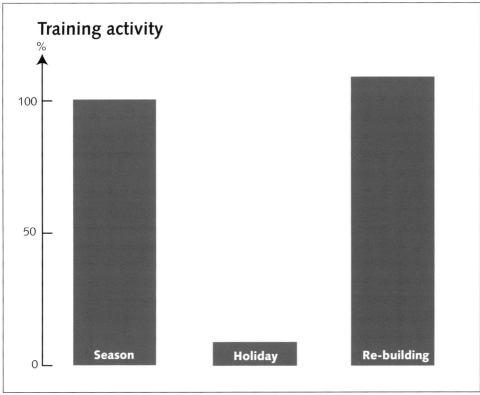

Figure PL12
The figure shows the training activities of a group of Danish elite players before, during, and after a three-week holiday. The values are expressed in relation to the activity level before the holiday (100%). The level of physical activity decreased markedly during the holidays, whereas the activity level was slightly higher during the re-building period compared to before the holiday period.

The results from the study are illustrated in Figs. PL10 (see page 189) and PL13 (see page 194). As expected, the three-week holiday caused a considerable decrease in performance capacity, but after the four-week re-building period the players performed better in a high-intensity exercise test compared to before the holiday period (see Fig. PL10). However, after the re-building period the endurance capacity had not returned to the level before the break (see Fig. PL13, page 194).

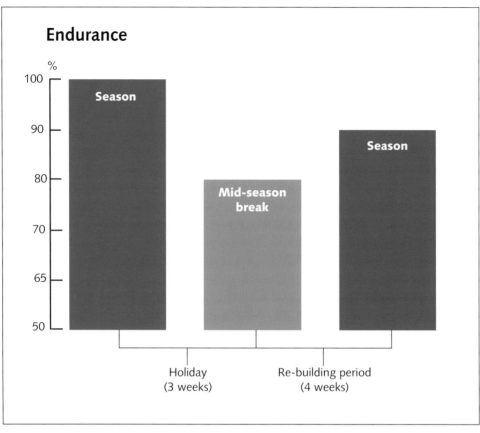

Figure PL13

The figure shows the endurance capacity of a group of Danish elite players during the season, after three weeks of holiday, and after a four-week re-building period (start of the second half of the season) (see Fig. PL12, page 193). The values are expressed in relation to the level during the season (100%).

The holiday caused a marked reduction in the endurance level, and a four-week re-building period was not sufficiently long for the players to return to the endurance capacity they had during the season.

The study showed that three weeks of very little physical activity is too long to enable the players to regain endurance capacity to the start of the second half of the season. Therefore, the players should perform aerobic moderate-intensity training during the maintenance period of a mid-season break. For psychological reasons it may be suitable for the players to be away from the club during the first part of the break and train on their own.

This training will facilitate the transition between the two periods and at the same time reduce the risk of injuries. In addition, more time will be available to train other aspects of the game during the re-building period. As in the pre-season period, the amount and intensity of the fitness training should be increased gradually during the re-building period.

Detailed planning

An example of the training frequency and exercise intensity of a typical week during the maintenance period in the mid-season break is illustrated in Scheme PL6 (the total duration of a training session is approximately 60 minutes).

The intensity of the training is represented by a number (1-5). A higher number means a higher intensity.

Week Schedule – Maintenance period

Day/Time period	0-15	15-30	30-45	45-60	minutes
Monday	Warm-up	4	3	3	Recovery activities
Wednesday	Warm-up	3	4	3	Recovery activities
Friday	Warm-up	3	4	3	Recovery activities

Scheme PL6

An example of the training frequency and intensity of a typical week for a non-professional team during the re-building period is illustrated in Scheme PL7 (the total duration of a training session is approximately 90 minutes).

Week Schedule – Rebuilding period

Day/Time period	0-15	15-30	30-45	45-60	60-75	75-90	minutes
Monday	Warm-up	3	3	4	3	3	Recovery activities
Tuesday	Warm-up	3	5	5	4	3	Recovery activities
Thursday	Warm-up	3	5	2	4	3	Recovery activities
Saturday	Warm-up			Match			

Scheme PL7
Explanation of codes:
2 = Low intensity, 3 = Moderate intensity
4 = High intensity, 5 = Very high intensity

| | Mid-season break | |
	Maintenance period	Re-building period
Aerobic		
Moderate-intensity training	444*	4433
High-intensity training	333	4555
Anaerobic		
**Speed endurance training	111	3544
Speed training	223	4555

Scheme PL8
Explanations of codes:
1 = Very low priority (need not be trained).
2 = Low priority (may be trained).
3 = Moderate priority (should preferably be trained).
4 = High priority (should be trained).
5 = Very high priority (must be trained).
* See book
** See book

Summary – mid-season break

The mid-season break can be divided into a maintenance period and a re-building period. It is important that the players are active during the maintenance period to ensure a gradual transition between the two periods. Towards the start of the second half of the season high-intensity training should be emphasised. Scheme PL8 shows an example of how much priority should be given to each form of training during a seven-week mid-season break. The higher the number (1-5), the more important the type of training.

Periods of reduced training

In some tournaments matches are played frequently, e.g. more than twice per week. In addition, teams are often taking part in several tournaments at the same time. During the season there may be cup matches and, for the top class teams, international games. In order to optimise the performance of the players the physical loading of some of the players during training may have to be reduced, so as not to „overtrain" these players. In this section an emphasis will be put on how to reduce the training load without lowering the performance level of the players. To share light on that issue a number of scientific studies focusing on the effect of a reduction in the amount of training will be discussed.

In a series of studies the effect of reduced training was investigated by reducing the amount of training during a 15-week period (R-training) after

In periods of the season the players can benefit from having light and enjoyable training sessions.

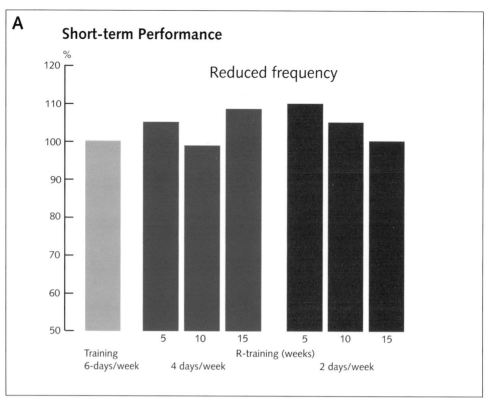

A

Short-term Performance

Reduced frequency

Figure PL14

The figure shows short-term performance determined as time to exhaustion (within 6 minutes) on an intense exercise test. Values during a 15-week reduced-training period (R-training) are given and expressed in relation to the level after a 10-week training period (Training). (A) One group reduced the training frequency from 6 to 4 times per week (left) and another group reduced the training frequency from 6 times to twice per week (right). Despite the reduced training frequency both groups were able to maintain performance. (B) One group reduced the duration of each training session from 40 to 26 min and another group reduced the duration of each training session from 40 to 13 min. Despite the reduced training duration neither groups had a decrease in performance. (C) One group reduced the intensity of training to 2/3 of the intensity during the training period (left) and another group reduced the intensity of training to 1/3 of the intensity during the training period (right). Both groups that reduced the intensity of training showed a decrease in performance

first having trained during a 10-week period with a frequency of 6 times per week, each session lasting 45 min (Training). In one group the frequency was reduced to 4 times per week, and in another group to twice per week. It was observed that performance in a short-term running test was not altered in either group during the 15 weeks of reduced training frequency (Fig. PL14A). In another study the frequency of training was maintained but the duration of the training sessions was reduced from 45 min to either 26 or to

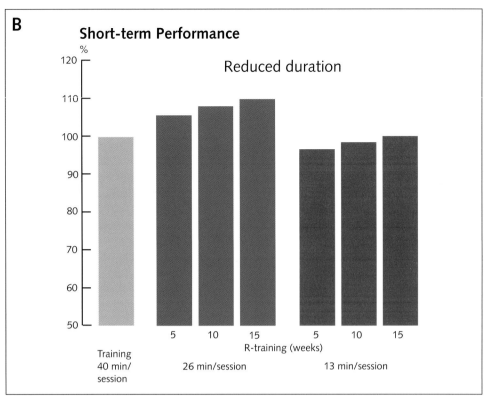

B

Short-term Performance

Reduced duration

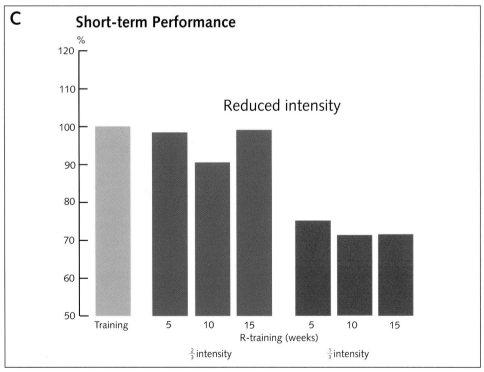

C

Short-term Performance

Reduced intensity

13 min in two groups, respectively. Neither short- nor long-term performance was changed during 15 weeks (Fig. PL14B). In a third experiment the intensity of training was reduced to $2/3$ and $1/3$ of the intensity the subject used during the 10-weeks of training, whereas the training duration and frequency was maintained. In the $1/3$ -intensity group short-term performance was lowered already after 5 weeks (Fig. PL14C), whereas in the $2/3$ -intensity group maximum oxygen uptake was reduced after 10 weeks of detraining. Both groups showed an impaired performance in an endurance tests after 15 weeks of detraining.

These experiments show that the frequency and the duration of the training can be reduced for a period of time without having any significant impact on the physical capacity, whereas a reduction in intensity of the training has a considerable effect on performance. Thus, it is important to maintain a high intensity during the training sessions, i.e. aerobic high-intensity and speed endurance training, in periods where the total amount of training is reduced. In general, in contrast to popular believes, it is beneficial to perform some high intensity training for a short period of time rather than no training. For example, two days before a game it is appropriate to perform a 20-min aerobic high-intensity training session.

Preparation for a tournament

Many teams are taking part in a tournament before or after a season. The preparation for and participation in such a competition should be carefully considered. To provide some general recommendations World Cup will be used as an example, since it is one of the longest lasting tournaments and often has a long preparation phase.

For the World Cup in soccer the performance level of the players not only has to be optimal at the start of the tournament for the qualification to the final rounds, but also throughout the entire tournament lasting up to six weeks. Thus, careful planning is required both for the preparation and for the tournament period.

A key question is when to bring the players together in the preparation for the World Cup. There is no unanimous answer to that question since there are many factors, of which the psychological aspects may be the most important. Traditionally the players are brought together 5-6 weeks before the World Cup. However, the winning of the Danish team in the 1992 European Championship with a only 10 days preparation period may get coaches to consider how to optimise the preparation for the World Cup. The preparation of the Danish team was definitely not optimal since some of the Danish players did not have a sufficient fitness level at the start of the tournament. On the other hand, the situation was advantageous in that the players did not become mentally exhausted, something that often happens for some of the players during a long lasting tournament after a long preparation period. There are many routes to success and each coach should decide upon the strategy for his team taking into account many factors, such

| | | Tournament preperation | | | | | | |
		Maintenance period		Re-building period				
Weeks*		7	6	5	4	3	2	1
Aerobic								
Moderate intensity training		5	5	3	3	3	3	2
Hing intensity training		2	2	3	4	5	4	2
Anaerobic								
**Speed endurance training		2	2	3	4	5	4	2
Speed training		2	3	4	5	5	4	4

Scheme PL9
Explanations of codes:
1 = Very low priority (need not be trained).
2 = Low priority (may be trained).
3 = Moderate priority (should preferably be trained).
4 = High priority (should be trained).
5 = Very high priority (must be trained).
* Weeks before the tournament*

as the need for tactical development, optimising the fitness level of the players, tradition and psychology.

Nevertheless, there are some general aspects to consider for the preparation and for the tournament period. The preparation period is divided into a maintenance and a rebuilding period, the latter being of a duration of five weeks. A suggestion for the priorities of the different types of fitness training during the preparation period is given in scheme PL9, assuming a 2-week maintenance period and a 5-week rebuilding period.

Maintenance period

The maintenance period represents the period from the end of the season to the start of the rebuilding period. The duration of the maintenance period may differ, not only between countries but also between players on the same team. In most countries several members of the national team are playing in other countries. Thus, the season of the players ends at different times. The players with an early end of the season have the advantage that they have a longer time to relax mentally from the season. On the other hand, they have a greater risk of a significant reduction of their physical capacity. Therefore, these players should, preferably together, undergo a fitness training programme during the maintenance period (see below). The players who end the season late also need to recover mentally before starting the intense part of the preparation for the World Cup. Therefore they should have a break, but without allowing for a major decrease in their physical capacity.

It is well known that in a period with reduced training there is little change in maximum oxygen uptake, whereas there is a marked and rapid reduction in the level of muscle endurance enzymes, which are closely associated with a decrease in the endurance capacity (see Fig. PL13, page 194). Furthermore, it takes quite a long time to re-establish the muscle endurance capacity. Thus, it is important to maintain the level of muscle endurance enzymes during the maintenance period to be able to reach an optimal fitness level at the start of the World Cup. This can best be done by performing aerobic moderate-intensity training. For a top-class soccer player training sessions of a duration of 45-60 minutes, 3-4 times a week are in most cases sufficient.

It is recommend that muscle strength and muscle endurance training is performed only to a minimal extent during the maintenance period (for further information see the book „Specific Muscle Training in Soccer").

Rebuilding period
During the rebuilding period aerobic high intensity training and anaerobic training should be emphasised (see Scheme PL9). The demand of the players should be increased slowly during the first three weeks with a limited priority on anaerobic training during the first week. The last week before the start of the World Cup the training load should be reduced, and mainly aerobic high intensity and speed training are to be performed (Scheme PL9).

The programme of fitness training during the rebuilding period leaves plenty of space for tactical and technical training. It is rare that a national coach can keep the players together for weeks, and it is a unique opportunity to work with tactical aspects, such as set-pieces and attacking strategies.

It is advantageous to play a couple of games at the highest possible competitive level during the rebuilding period since some of the players may not have played a competitive game for over four weeks. The matches may be played at the end of the second week and in the middle of the fourth week of the rebuilding period, i.e. 3 and 1 1/2 week before the World Cup. Along with the importance of improving the physical capacity of the players, the matches are also useful for practising tactical strategies and for re-establishing the technical level.

A group of players that need special attention in the rebuilding period are those that do not play regularly on the team. Often the physical load on these players is not sufficiently high. In a study of a Danish team preparing for a European quarter final during off-season, it was observed that only players that played regularly on the team had a significant improvement in maximum oxygen uptake and performance during the preparation period (see Fig. PL15). Therefore, it is of value to play a couple of matches during the preparation period, with players who are not regularly playing on the team.

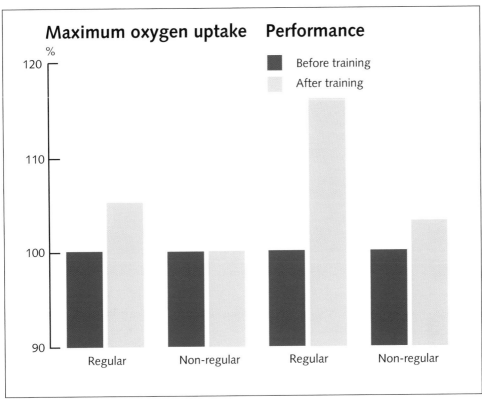

Figure PL15
The figure shows maximum oxygen uptake and performance of intense exercise for regular and non-regular first team players before (■ *) and after (* ▨ *) a 7-week preparation period for a European Cup quarter-final match. Note that only the regular players had improvements.*

Tournament period

It is often believed that it is not necessary to perform fitness training once the tournament is started. However, this is not true. In general, the day after a match the players that have taken part in a major fraction of the game should perform aerobic low-intensity training. The following day they may do aerobic high-intensity training for 20-30 minutes and, occasionally, speed training. The next day, if this is the day before the next match, only aerobic low-intensity training should be performed, and it is recommended that the duration of the training session is maximally 60 minutes. These are general guidelines, but individual needs should be considered, e.g. if a player appears to be overloaded, the demand on the player should be reduced.

For the players that did not participate in the game or only played a minor part of the game, training the day after a game should be physically demanding. It should mainly consist of aerobic high-intensity training and short periods of anaerobic speed endurance training. It is important to be aware of the need to maintain the reserve players at a high fitness level since

	Pre-season	Season	Break	Season
Aerobic training				
Moderate-intensity	3344 4444 4455 4443	4343 4343 433	4 4444 33 43	4343 4343 4343
High-intensity	2223 3234 4445 4555	5555 5555 555	3 3345 55 55	5555 5555 5444
Anaerobic training				
*Speed endurance	1111 1111 2334 4555	3453 4534 543	1 1135 44 53	4534 5345 3453
Speed	1111 1111 2344 4555	5555 5555 555	2 2345 55 55	5555 5555 5544

Scheme PL10

Explanations of codes:

1 = Very low priority (need not be trained).

2 = Low priority (may be trained).

3 = Moderate priority (should preferably be trained).

4 = High priority (should be trained).

5 = Very high priority (must be trained).

* See book

some of these individuals may become key players during the final rounds of the World Cup as a result of injuries and quarantines of players within the team.

As for the preparation period muscle strength and muscle endurance training should only to a minor extent be carried out during the tournament.

Summary

Scheme PL10 evaluates the priority of the different types of fitness training during various periods of the year. The higher the number (1-5), the more important the form of training. The scheme is based on an eight-month season with a seven-week mid-season break (for practical reasons each month is assumed to have four weeks).

The planning of training is dependent upon the level of competition. Fitness training for recreational players that train a couple of times per week should mainly focus on aerobic moderate- and high-intensity training as well as anaerobic speed training. Players that are training more often should also emphasise anaerobic speed endurance training. For elite players, fitness training should also include specific muscle training, particularly muscle strength training (see the book „Specific Muscle Training in Soccer").

The needs of each individual player should be taken into account. Players that are not playing regularly on a team should be paid special attention and they should perform more fitness training than the other players.

In periods with many matches or periods where players are physically and mentally overloaded, the amount of training can be reduced. It is, however, important that the players frequently perform aerobic high-intensity training and, for top-class players, anaerobic speed endurance training.

In preparation for a tournament the players should perform aerobic moderate-intensity exercise in the maintenance period. In the following re-building period they should mainly perform aerobic high-intensity exercise and anaerobic training. During the tournament the amount of fitness training can be reduced. Nevertheless, frequent sessions with aerobic high-intensity training are recommended.

Word index

References and further reading

Books

Handbook of Sports Medicine and Science. Football (Soccer) (1994). Ed.: Ekblom B. Blackwell Scientific Publications, London/Boston.

Science and Football (1988). Eds.: Reilly T., Lees A., Davids K. & Murphy W.J. E. & F.N. Spon, London/New York.

Science and Football II (1993). Eds.: Reilly T., Clarys J. & Stibbe A. E. & F.N. Spon, London/New York.

Science and Football III (1996). Eds.: Reilly T., Bangsbo J. & Hughes M. E & F.N. Spon, London/New York.

The Physiology of Soccer - with Special Reference to Intense Intermittent Exercise. (1994). Bangsbo J. HO+Storm, Brudelysvej 26, Bagsvaerd, Denmark (Fax. +4544981766), pp. 1-155. Available in English, Italian, Spanish & French.

Fitness Training in Football a Scientific Approach" (1994). Bangsbo, J. HO+Storm, Bagsværd, Denmark Denmark (Fax. +4544981766), pp. 1-325. Available in English, Spanish, Italian, Polish, Macedonia, Greek, Turkish, Swedish & Danish.

The Child and Adolescent Athlete (1996). Ed: Bar-Or, O. IOC Encyclopaedia volume. Blackwell Scientific Publications, London/Boston.

Soccer & Science (2000). Ed: Bangsbo, J. Munksgaard & Institute of Exercise and Sport Sciences, University of Copenhagen/Munksgaard, pp. 1-151.

Soccer Systems & Strategies (2000). Bangsbo J. & Peitersen, B. Human Kinetics. P.O.Box 5076, Champaign, IL 61825-5076, USA.

Articles

Bangsbo J. (1990). Usefulness of blood lactate measurements in soccer. Science and Football 3: 2-4.

Bangsbo J. (1992). Anaerobic energy yield in soccer - performance of young players. Science and Football 5: 24-28.

Bangsbo J. (1992). Time motion characteristics of competition soccer. Science and Football 6: 21-25.

Bangsbo J., Nørregaard L. & Thorsøe F. (1991). Activity profile of competition soccer. Canadian Journal of Sport Sciences 16: 110-116.

Bangsbo J. & Lindquist F. (1992). Comparison of various exercise tests with endurance performance during soccer in professional players. International Journal of Sports Medicine 13: 125-132.

Bangsbo J., Nørregaard L. & Thorsøe F. (1992). The effect of carbohydrate diet on intermittent exercise performance. International Journal of Sports Medicine 13: 152-157.

Bangsbo J., Petersen A. & Michalsik L. (1992). Accumulated O_2 deficit during intense exercise and muscle characteristics of elite athletes. International Journal of Sports Medicine 14: 207-213.

Bangsbo J. (1994). „Fitness training in soccer." In: „Football (Soccer)", ed. B. Ekblom, Blackwell/IOC, pp. 124-138.

Bangsbo J. (1994). Soccer specific endurance. Science and Football 8: 20-21, 1994.

Bangsbo J. (1995). „Physiology of training". In: „Science and Soccer" ed. T. Reilly. London, New York, E. & F.N. Spon Publ., pp. 51-64.

Bangsbo J. (1995). Energy demands in soccer. Brucosport, Brugge, 13-14 October, 9-13.

Bangsbo J. (1996). Yo-Yo tests of practical endurance and recovery for soccer. Performance Conditioning Soccer, USA, 2: 8.

Bangsbo, J. (1998). Optimal preparation for the world cup in soccer. Clinics in Sports Medicine 14: 697-709.

Bangsbo, J. (1998). Medically fit: Yes, Match fit? In: Medicine Matters, UEFA Technical Department 1.

Bangsbo, J. (1999). Physiology of intermittent exercise. In: Exercise: Basic and Applied Science. Eds W. E. Garrett & D. Kirkendall, Williams Wilkins, USA, pp. 53-66.

Bangsbo, J. (1999). Team Sports. In: „Nutrition in Sports."
IOC Encyclopaedia volume. Blackwell Science, pp 563-571.

Berg K.E., La Voie, J.C. & Latin, R.W. (1985). Physiological training effects of playing youth soccer. Medicine and Science in Sports and Exercise 17: 656-660.

Boobis L.H. (1987). Metabolic aspects of fatigue during sprinting.
In: Macleod D., Maughan R., Nimmo M., Reilly T. & Williams T.C. (eds). Exercise; Benefits, Limits and Adaptations, E. & F.N. Spon, London/New York pp. 116-143.

Ekstrand J. (1982). Soccer injuries and their prevention (thesis). Linkoping University Medical Dissertation 130, Linkoping, Sweden.

Hansen, L., Bangsbo, J., Twisk, J. & Klausen, K. (1999). Development of muscle strength in relation to training level and testosterone in young male soccer players. J. Appl. Physiol. 3:1141-1147.

Hansen, L, Klausen, K. Bangsbo, J. & Müller, J. (1999). Short longitudinal study of boys playing soccer: Parenthal height, birth weight and length, anthropometry, and pubertal maturation in elite and non-elite players. Pediatric Exercise Science 11:199-207.

Hickson R.C., Foster C., Polloack M.L., Galassi T.M. & Rich S. (1985) Reduced training intensities and loss of aerobic power, endurance, and cardiac growth. Journal of Applied Physiology 58: 492-499.

Reilly T. (1990). Football. In: Reilly, T., Secher N., Snell P. & Williams C. (eds). Physiology of Sports, E.& F.N. Spon, London/New York, pp. 465-487.

Reilly T. & Bangsbo J. (1998). Anaerobic and aerobic training. In: „Applied Sport Science: Training in Sport". Ed. B. Elliott, Australia, pp. 351-409.

www.soccerfitness.com

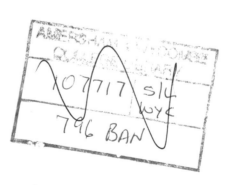

Buckinghamshire College Group
Wycombe Campus